ISLAMIC ECONOMICS AND FINANCE

A BIBLIOGRAPHY

ISLAMIC ECONOMICS AND FINANCE

A BIBLIOGRAPHY

COMPILED BY

JAVED AHMAD KHAN

MANSELL

First published 1995 by
Mansell Publishing Limited, *A Cassell imprint*
Villiers House, 41/47 Strand, London WC2N 5JE, England
387 Park Avenue South, New York, New York 10016–8810, USA

British Library Cataloguing in Publication Data
Islamic Economics and Finance: Bibliography
I. Khan, Javed Ahmad
016.3300917671
ISBN 0–7201–2219–8

Library of Congress Cataloging-in-Publication Data
Khan, Javed Ahmad.
Islamic economics and finance : a bibliography / compiled by Javed Ahmad Khan.
p. cm.
'A Cassell imprint'
Includes bibliographical references and index.
ISBN 0–7201–2219–8 : $80.00
1. Economics–Islamic countries–Bibliography. 2. Finance–Islamic countries–Bibliography. 3. Islamic countries–Economic conditions–Bibliography. 4. Economics–Religious aspects–Islam–Bibliography. I. Title.
Z7164.E2K497 1995
[HB126.4]
016.330917'671–dc20 94–20928
CIP

Printed and bound in Great Britain by Biddles Ltd, Guildford and King's Lynn

CONTENTS

PREFACE

It is now widely acknowledged that Islamic economics is one of the most significant aspects of Islamic resurgence in the Muslim world and has attracted increasing attention in recent years. Its development during the last two and a half decades has been so impressive that it has become extremely difficult to keep pace with the growing literature coming out in all parts of the world. It has aroused such a worldwide interest that scholars have endeavoured to explore almost every aspect of Islamic economics. Islamic economics has now taken on a highly developed form. The proponent of this system also provides an Islamic critique of economic systems and theories. As a result, a number of research centres are already engaged in educative efforts and Islamic economics is taught as a discipline in the universities of both Islamic and non-Muslim countries.

The purpose of this bibliography is to provide an up-to-date collection of source materials on the subject of Islamic economics written in the English language during the last two decades. The focus is on contemporary literature; however, the bibliography also includes the historical accounts of Islamic economy that researchers may require for background materials. This bibliography has been prepared to serve as a useful research tool for individual researchers, libraries, centres of Islamic studies, and for research institutes concerned with development in the theory and practice of Islamic economics and finance.

Some good-quality literature surveys and well researched bibliographies on Islamic economics have appeared during the last ten years. For example, *Muslim Economic Thinking: A Survey of Contemporary Literature* by Professor M.N. Siddiqi came out in 1981 and covered the three major languages of Arabic, Urdu and English. Then in 1982, a German economist, Dr Volker Nienhaus, published *Literature on Islamic Economics in English and German*, focusing on the practical side of

Islamic economics. Following this, Muhammad Akram Khan's *Islamic Economics: Annotated Sources in English and Urdu* (1983) covered about seven hundred entries. Another work, *Islamic Economics: A Bibliography*, was published in 1984 by the Islamic Research and Training Institute, Islamic Development Bank, Jeddah, and its compiler, Tariqullah Khan, collected more than six hundred entries in the English language. Finally, Akhtar A. Siddiqui's *A Bibliography on Islamic Banking* (1985), published in Pakistan, was exclusively devoted to Islamic banking institutions. Since then, particularly between the years 1985 and 1993, there has been an absolute boom in writings on Islamic economics and the existing bibliographies could not keep up with the output. Thus the existing bibliographies on Islamic economics cover the period until 1985; the present bibliography covers the period up to 1993. As a matter of fact, many people are unaware of the amount of research work being done in the field of Islamic economic systems. This bibliography provides the source of information for researchers interested in Islamic economics in the English language only.

Coverage

The bibliography consists of some 1,600 entries related to the contemporary works on Islamic economics and finance dealing with issues such as the philosophy of the Islamic economic system, the economic history of the Muslim people, the concept of economic development and growth in Islam, the theory and practice of Islamic financial institutions, the monetary and fiscal policy of Islam, and Islamic commercial laws.

The selection of items has been drawn from a wide range of published and unpublished material, which includes books, articles, doctoral dissertations, papers presented at seminars and conferences, and bibliographies. The important researches of early writers, including classical works on Islamic economics and finance, have also been incorporated in order to present the subject in its historical perspective.

Sources

I have collected most of these materials from my personal research work in the Aligarh Muslim University during the last decade and from the wealth of unpublished materials available in the university and elsewhere. While preparing this bibliography, an attempt was made to consult all the available sources. Most of these materials are drawn from a number of Islamic economics journals and other periodicals (see the

Appendix). Moreover, I have benefited from some books which had separate bibliographical listings. In this regard, M. Umar Chapra's *Islam and the Economic Challenge*, Mohammad Anwar's *Modelling Interest-Free Economy* and Zafarul Islam's *A Bibliography of Islamic Law in English* are worth mentioning. The reader will find that a number of such entries may also appear in the other bibliographies on Islamic economics mentioned earlier.

Arrangement

The bibliography is divided into two parts: *Islamic Economic Systems* and *Money, Banking and Finance*. Each part is arranged under general subjects and subdivided by themes. Within each section, entries are arranged alphabetically by author or, if there is no author, by title. Each entry aims to give name of author(s), editor(s), title, edition or volume when relevant, place of publication, publisher, date of publication and number of pages. In some cases, however, it was not always possible to give the fullest information. Entries are numbered sequentially throughout the bibliography. An appendix of the important serial publications which are exclusively devoted to the theory and practice of Islamic economics is also provided, giving a brief description, aims and objectives, and full addresses for those wishing to make further study in the field. There are separate author and subject indexes; references are to entry numbers, not pages.

This bibliography makes no claim to completeness, but the material listed should provide a comprehensive list of contemporary research works on the fast-growing discipline of Islamic economics and finance.

ACKNOWLEDGEMENTS

This bibliography is the result of a research project undertaken in 1990, in the Centre of West Asian Studies, Aligarh Muslim University, Aligarh, India.

The essential work was made possible thanks to the assistance of Professor Mahmudal Huq, my doctoral adviser, whose encouragement to search out and identify the Islamic economics materials helped to provide an important focus for this work. It is to him, first and foremost, that my deepest appreciation and gratitude is due.

I am grateful to Professor Akhtar Majeed, Director of the Centre, for his many-sided support and co-operation and to my colleagues at the Centre for encouraging me in this venture. This work could not have been completed without their advice, help and moral support through my years of research there. I also wish to thank the staff members of the Centre's library who provided all possible assistance at every stage of the work.

My appreciation is also due to some individuals who have assisted me in the collection of materials and information over many years. Among them are Dr F.R. Faridi of the Institute of Objective Studies and Dr A.A. Islahi of the Department of Economics at Aligarh Muslim University, and Professor M.N. Siddiqi of the Centre for Research in Islamic Economics, King Abdul Aziz University, Saudi Arabia.

The patience and encouragement of my parents and family helped to ease me through the research for this work.

I must acknowledge with thanks the help of my son, Mohammed Abdullah, in typing many parts of this work after his class work and I am grateful to Mr Asim Ali and Mr Shoaib Ahamd for word-processing the entire work. My gratitude is also due to Afzal Mushahdi for his invaluable guidance and encouragement.

To
my mother and father

Part I

ISLAMIC ECONOMIC SYSTEMS

I

GENERAL SOURCES ON ISLAMIC ECONOMICS

Teaching and Research

1 ABU-SAUD, Mahmoud, 'Critique of teaching economics in an Islamic perspective', in S. Tahir *et al.* (eds.), *Readings in Microeconomics: An Islamic Perspective*, Petaling Jaya: Longman Malaysia, 1992, pp. 24–30.

2 AHMAD, Khurshid *et al.*, 'Problems of research in Islamic economics with emphasis on research administration and finance', in *Problems of Research in Islamic Economics*, Research Papers and Proceedings, Amman: Royal Academy for Islamic Civilization Research (Al-Albait Foundation), 1987, pp. 75–105.

3 AHMAD, Khurshid *et al.*, *Problems of Research in Islamic Economics*, A symposium jointly held with the Islamic Research and Training Institute, Islamic Development Bank, Jeddah, Saudi Arabia, 1986, Amman: Royal Academy for Islamic Civilization Research (Al-Albait Foundation), 1987, pp. 28–38.

4 *Announcement on Research Proposal*, Jeddah: International Centre for Research in Islamic Economics, King Abdul Aziz University, 1983.

5 *Annual Report, 1986–87*, Islamabad: International Institute of Islamic Economics, International Islamic University, 1987, 38 pp.

6 ARIFF, Muhammad, 'Towards a more effective way of teaching and studying economics: a focus on the basics', *Muslim Education Quarterly* (Cambridge), Vol. 8, No. 2, 1991, pp. 27–31.

7 EL-BDOUR, Radi *et al.*, 'Problems of research in Islamic economics with emphasis on priorities and application', in *Problems of Research in Islamic Economics*, Research Papers and

Proceedings, Amman: Royal Academy for Islamic Civilization Research (Al-Albait Foundation), 1987, pp. 107–44.

8 DERAKHSHAN, Masoud, 'Islamic economics: teaching and research – a report from Iran', *Journal of Objective Studies* (Aligarh), Vol. 2, No. 1, 1990, pp. 32–45.

9 'Guidelines for key issues in Islamic economics', Jeddah: International Centre for Research in Islamic Economics, 1985.

10 GUL, Abdullah and DOHA, S., *Economic Research Institutions of the Islamic World*, Jeddah: Islamic Research and Training Institute, Islamic Development Bank, 1984, 132 pp.

11 *International Islamic University, Institute of Islamic Economics, Regulation for Graduate Progress leading to M.Sc. and Ph.D. in Economics, 1986–87*, Islamabad: International Islamic University, 1987, 101 pp.

12 Islamic Research and Training Institute, Islamic Development Bank, New Pusu, *Economic Research Institutions of the Islamic World*, Jeddah: Islamic Research and Training Institute, Islamic Development Bank, 1984.

13 KHAN, M. Fahim, Review article on *Directory of Islamic Financial Institutions* ed. John R. Presley, in *Muslim World Book Review* (Leicester), Vol. 9, No. 3, 1989, p. 34.

14 KHAN, Tariqullah, *Teaching Programmes in Islamic Economics – A Review*, Jeddah: Islamic Research and Training Institute, 1989, 38 pp.

15 MANNAN, M.A., *Abstracts of Researches in Islamic Economics*, Jeddah: International Centre for Research in Islamic Economics, King Abdul Aziz University, 1984, 87 pp.

16 'Monetary and fiscal economics of Islam: an outline of some major subjects for research', in Mohammad Ariff (ed.), *Monetary and Fiscal Economics of Islam*, Jeddah: International Centre for Research in Islamic Economics, King Abdul Aziz University, 1982, pp. 375–86.

17 *Ninth Annual Report of the Islamic Research and Training Institute, 1990–1991*, Jeddah: Islamic Development Bank, 1992, 93 pp.

18 *Problems of Research in Islamic Economics*, Jeddah: Islamic Research and Training Institute, Islamic Development Bank, 1987.

19 SARDAR, Z. and MANZOOR, S.P., 'Disciplines at turning points: the new undergraduate and postgraduate courses on offer at the International Institute of Islamic Economics in Islamabad', *Inquiry*, Vol. 3, No. 4, 1986, pp. 26–9.

20 SIDDIQI, M. Nejatullah, 'Some notes on teaching economics in an Islamic framework', in S. Tahir *et al.* (eds.), *Readings in Microeconomics: An Islamic Perspective*, Petaling Jaya: Longman Malaysia, 1992, pp. 1–23.

21 SIDDIQI, M. Nejatullah, 'Restructuring the study of economics in Muslim universities', in Islamil R. Al-Faruqi and Abdullah Omar Naseef, *Social and Natural Sciences: The Islamic Perspective*, Jeddah: King Abdul Aziz University, 1981.

22 'The Royal Academy for Islamic Civilization Research', in *Problems of Research in Islamic Economics*, Amman: Royal Academy for Islamic Civilization Research (Al-Albait Foundation), 1987.

23 YALCINTAS, Nevzet *et al.*, 'Problems of research in Islamic economics: general background', in *Problems of Research in Islamic Economics*, Research Papers and Proceedings, Amman: Royal Academy for Islamic Civilization Research (Al-Albait Foundation), 1987, pp. 21–50.

24 EL-ZARQA, Mohammad Anas *et al.*, 'Problems of research in the theory of Islamic economics and suggested solutions', *Problems of Research in Islamic Economics*, Research Papers and Proceedings, Amman: Royal Academy for Islamic Civilization Research (Al-Albait Foundation), 1987, pp. 51–74.

Bibliographies and Glossaries

25 KHAN, Muhammad Akram, *Islamic Economics: Annotated Sources in English and Urdu*, Leicester: Islamic Foundation, 1983

26 KHAN, M. Akram, *Glossary of Islamic Economics*, London: Mansell, 1990, 144 pp.

27 KHAN, Tariqullah, *Islamic Economics: A Bibliography*, Jeddah: Islamic Research and Training Institute, Islamic Development Bank, 1984.

28 PRESLEY, J.R., 'Selected bibliography on Islamic economics and banking', in John R. Presley (ed.), *Directory of Islamic Financial Institutions*, London: Croom Helm, 1988, pp. 78–96.

29 SIDDIQUI, Akhtar A., *A Bibliography on Islamic Banking*, Karachi: Islamic Documentation and Information Centre, 1985, 27 pp.

30 TORREY, Charles C., *The Commercial–Theological Terms in the Koran*, Leiden: Brill, 1892, 51 pp.

31 ZAMAN, Hasanuz S.M., 'A glossary of classical Islamic terms', *Islamic Order* (Karachi), Vol. 1, No. 1, 1979, pp. 61–8.

Literature Surveys

32 HOSSEINI, Hamid, 'Notions of private property in Islamic economics in contemporary Iran: a review of literature', *International Journal of Social Economics*, Vol. 15, No. 9, 1988, pp. 51–61.

33 KHAN, M. Akram, 'A survey of contemporary Islamic thought on the institution of interest', *Islamic Education* (Lahore), Vol. 6, No. 4, 1973.

34 KHAN, M. Akram, 'A survey of critical literature on interest-free banking', *Journal of Islamic Banking and Finance* (Karachi), Vol. 6, No. 1, 1989, pp. 45–61.

35 SIDDIQI, M. Nejatullah, *Muslim Economic Thinking: A Survey of Contemporary Literature*, Leicester: Islamic Foundation, for the International Centre for Research in Islamic Economics, King Abdul Aziz University, Jeddah, 1981.

36 SIDDIQI, M. Nejatullah, 'Recent works on history of economic thought in Islam: a survey', in A.H.M. Sadeq and A. Ghazali (eds.), *Readings in Islamic Economic Thought*, Petaling Jaya: Longman Malaysia, 1992, pp. 33–58.

2

NATURE AND CONCEPT OF ISLAMIC ECONOMICS

Definition of Islamic Economics

37 ABU-SAUD, Mahmoud, 'Towards Islamic economics', in *Toward Islamization of Disciplines*, Herndon, VA: International Institute of Islamic Thought, 1989, pp. 265–70.

38 AHMAD, Khurshid, 'Nature and significance of Islamic economics', in A. Ahmad and K.R. Awan (eds.), *Lectures on Islamic Economics*, Jeddah: Islamic Development Bank, 1992, pp. 19–48.

39 ARIFF, Muhammad, 'Towards a definition of Islamic economics: some scientific considerations', *Journal of Research in Islamic Economics*, Vol. 2, Winter 1985, pp. 87–103.

40 ARIFF, Muhammad, 'Towards the Shariah paradigm of Islamic economics: the beginning of a scientific revolution', *The American Journal of Islamic Social Sciences*, Vol. 2, July 1985, pp. 79–99.

41 FARIDI, F.R., 'Defining Islamic economics', *Islamic Economics News Bulletin* (Aligarh), Vol. 3, No. 2, 1993, p. 1.

42 KATOUZIAN, Homa, 'Shi'ism and Islamic economics: Sadr and Bani Sadr', in N. Keddie (ed.), *Religion and Politics in Iran: Shi'ism from Quietism to Revolution*, New Haven, CT: Yale University Press, 1983.

43 KHAN, M. Akram, 'Islamic economics: nature and need', *Journal of Research in Islamic Economics*, Vol. 1, No. 2, 1984, pp. 55–62.

44 MANNAN, M.A., *Why is Islamic Economics Important? Seven Reasons for Believing*, Jeddah: International Centre for Research in Islamic Economics, 1982.

45 ZAMAN, Hasanuz, 'Definition of Islamic economics', *Journal of Research in Islamic Economics*, Vol. 1, No. 2, 1984, pp. 51–4.

Principles and Philosophy

46 ABBASI, Sami M., HOLLMAN, K.W. and MURREY, J.H., 'Islamic economics: foundations and practices', *International Journal of Social Economics*, Vol. 16, No. 5, 1989, pp. 5–17.

47 ABDUL-RAUF, Muhammad, 'The ten commandments of Islamic economics', *Across the Board*, Vol. 18, August 1979, pp. 8–19.

48 AHMAD, Khurshid, 'Islam and simple living', *Criterion* (Karachi), July–August 1970, pp. 5–12.

49 AHMAD, S. Mahmud, *Economics of Islam*, Lahore: Ashraf, 1952.

50 ALI, Ausaf, 'The concept of spending in Islamic economics', *The Universal Message* (Karachi), Vol. 11, No. 6, 1989, pp. 31–4, 59.

51 Association of Muslim Social Scientists, *Outlines of Islamic Economics*, Proceedings of the First Symposium on the Economics of Islam in North America, March 1977.

52 BANI-SADR, Abdul Hasan, 'Islamic economics: ownership and Tawhid', in John J. Donohue and John L. Esposito (eds.), *Islam in Transition*, New York: Oxford University Press, 1982.

53 CHAPRA, M. Umer, *Objectives of the Islamic Economic Order*, Leicester: Islamic Foundation, 1979.

54 CHAPRA, M. Umer, *The Economic System of Islam – A Discussion of Its Goals and Nature*, London: Islamic Culture Centre, 1970.

55 CHOUDHURY, M.A., 'Principles of Islamic economics', *Islamic Studies*, Vol. 21, No. 2, 1982, pp. 89–107.

56 ISLAM, M. Zohurul, *Islamic Economics*, Dhaka: Islamic Foundation Bangladesh, 1987.

57 Islamic Economics Research Bureau, *Thoughts on Islamic Economics*, Dhaka: Islamic Economics Research Bureau, 1980.

58 JABBAR, M. Abdul, 'Philosophical Background of Islamic economics', *Thoughts on Economics* (Dhaka), Vol. 1, No. 1, 1991, pp. 64–7.

59 KHAN, M. Akram, *Economic Teachings of Prophet Muhammad (pbuh): A Select Anthology of Hadith Literature on Economics*, Islamabad: International Institute of Islamic Economics, 1989, 355 pp.

60 MAAMIRY, A. Hamoud Ali, *Economics in Islam*, New Delhi: Lancer, 1987.

61 MANNAN, M.A., 'The frontiers of Islamic economics: some philosophical underpinnings', in *Towards Islamization of Disciplines*, Herndon, VA: International Institute of Islamic Thought, 1989, pp. 295–311.

62 MUSLEHUDDIN, Muhammad, *Economics and Islam*, Lahore: Islamic Publications, 1974.

63 NAQVI, S.N.H., 'Economics of human rights: an Islamic perspective', *Hamdard Islamicus* (Karachi), Summer 1981, pp. 31–51.

64 NASR, Seyyed Vali Reza, 'Islamic economics: novel perspectives', *Middle Eastern Studies* (London), Vol. 25, No. 4, 1989, pp. 516–30.

65 NASR, Seyyed Vali Reza, 'Towards a philosophy of Islamic economics', *The Muslim World*, Vol. 77, No. 3–4, 1987, pp. 175–96.

66 PRYOR, Frederic L., 'The Islamic economic system', *Journal of Comparative Economics* (New York), Vol. 9, 1985, pp. 197–223.

67 RAHMAN, Afzalur, *Economic Doctrines of Islam*, Lahore: Islamic Publications, 1975.

68 SADEQ, A.H.M., *Islamic Economics*, Lahore: Islamic Publications, 1989, 180 pp.

69 SADR, Muhammad B., *Iqtisaduna*, English tr. by World Organization for Islamic Services, Tehran: 1982.

70 SALEM, Shehzad, 'An interest-free economy' (Pakistan), *Renaissance* (Lahore), Vol. 2, No. 5, 1992, pp. 3–12.

71 SANDEELA, Fateh M., 'Towards the Islamic economic order', *Islamic Order*, Vol. 8, No. 2, 1986, pp. 85–95.

72 SATOSHI, Iwai, *A New Approach to Human Economics: A Case Study of an Islamic Economy*, Working Paper No. 2, Japan: Institute of Middle East Studies, International University of Japan, June 1985.

73 SHAGHIL, M., 'Islamic economics: a view', *Journal of the West Asian Studies Society* (Aligarh), No. 2, 1986, pp. 11–15.

74 SHARRAF, B.A., 'The fundamentals and the possibilities', *Arabia* (London), October 1984, p. 44.

75 SIDDIQI, M. Nejatullah, *Some Aspects of the Islamic Economy*, Lahore: Islamic Publications, 1970.

76 TALIQANI, Ayatullah Mahmud, 'The characteristics of Islamic economics', in John J. Donohue and John L. Esposito (eds.), *Islam in Transition*, New York: Oxford University Press, 1982.

77 ZAIM, Sabahuddin, 'Islamic economics as a system based on human values', *Journal of Islamic Banking and Finance* (Karachi), No. 2, 1989, pp. 13–21.

78 ZARQA, M. Anas, 'Islamic economics: an approach to human welfare', in K. Ahmad (ed.), *Studies in Islamic Economics*, Leicester: Islamic Foundation, 1980, pp. 13–15.

Islamic Ethics and Economics

79 AHMAD, Syed Fayyaz, 'The ethical responsibility of business: Islamic principles and implications', *Journal of Objective Studies* (Aligarh), Vol. 3, No. 1, 1991, pp. 23–43.

80 ARIFF, Mohammad, 'Islamic ethics and economics', *Proceedings of the Seventh Annual Conference of AMSS (Association of Muslim Social Scientists [USA])*, Indianapolis, Indiana, 30 June – 1 July 1978.

81 BAYAT, Assef, 'The work ethic in Islam: a comparison with Protestantism', *The Islamic Quarterly* (London), Vol. 36, No. 1, 1992, pp. 5–27.

82 GAMBLING, Trevor and KARIM, Rifaat Ahmad Abdul, *Business and Accounting Ethics in Islam*, London: Mansell, 1991, 244 pp.

83 KHUMAWALA, Basheer, 'Economics, ethics and religion: the Islamic teachings', *The Message International* (Jamaica, NY), Vol. 14, No. 11, 1991, pp. 15–16.

84 MIKA'ILU, A.S., *Ethics and Business Performance: An Islamic Analysis*, Zaria, Nigeria: Usman Dan Fodio University, 1989, 82 pp.

85 NAQVI, S.N.H., *Ethics and Economics: An Islamic Synthesis*, Leicester: Islamic Foundation, 1981.

86 NAQVI, S.N.H., 'Ethical foundations of Islamic economics', *Islamic Studies*, Vol. 17, No. 2, 1978, pp. 105–36.

87 NAQVI, S.N.H., 'Islamic economic system: fundamental issues', *Islamic Studies*, Vol. 16, Winter 1977, pp. 327–46.

88 QUAZI, Naseem, 'Economic morality in Islam', *Hamdard Islamicus* (Karachi), Vol. 16, No. 4, 1993, pp. 89–102.

89 RAGIE, Zahier Ahmad, 'Some ethical principles of business as explained in the Sunnah', *Al-Balagh* (Karachi), Vol. 1, No. 9, 1991, pp. 13–16.

90 SATTAR, Zaidi, 'The ethics of profits in the Islamic economic system', *Islamic Quarterly*, Second quarter, 1988, pp. 69–76.

3

ISLAMIC ECONOMIC ALTERNATIVES

Methodology of Islamic Economics

91 ABU-ALI, Sultan, 'Islamic Economic System', in A. Ahmad and K.R. Awan (eds.), *Lectures on Islamic Economics*, Jeddah: Islamic Development Bank, 1992, pp. 131–44.

92 AHMAD, Ausaf and AWAN, Kazim Raza (eds.), *Lectures on Islamic Economics*, Jeddah: Islamic Development Bank, 1992, 473 pp.

93 ANWAR, Mohammad, 'Islamic economic methodology', *Journal of Objective Studies* (Aligarh), Vol. 2, No. 2, 1990, pp. 28–46.

94 ARIFF, Muhammad, 'Islamization of knowledge and some methodological issues in paradigm building: the general case of social science with a special focus on economics', *American Journal of Islamic Social Sciences*, Vol. 4, No. 1, 1979, p. 51.

95 GHAZALI, Aidit and OMAR, Syed (eds.), *Readings in the Concept and Methodology of Islamic Economics*, Selangor Darul Ehsan, Malaysia: Pelanduk Publications, 1989, 168 pp.

96 MANNAN, M.A., 'Islamic economics as a social science', *Journal of Research in Islamic Economics*, Vol. 1, No. 1, 1983, pp. 49–63.

97 NASR, Seyyed Vali Reza, 'Islam and the social sciences', *Hamdard Islamicus*, Vol. 13, No. 2, 1990, pp. 83–92.

98 SHARIF, M. Raihan, 'On methodology of Islamic economics', *Thoughts on Economics*, Vol. 8, No. 1, 1987, pp. 1–20.

99 ZARQA, Mohammad Anas, 'Methodology of Islamic economics', in A. Ahmad and K.R. Awan (eds.), *Lectures on Islamic Economics*, Jeddah: Islamic Development Bank, 1992, pp. 49–58.

General Objectives

100 AHMAD, Imtiaz Uddin, Review essay on *Islam and the Economic Challenge* by M. Umer Chapra, in *The American Journal of Islamic Social Sciences*, Vol. 9, No. 4, 1992, pp. 546–55.

101 ALI, Ausaf, 'In defence of and a plea for Islamic economics', *The Universal Message* (Karachi), Vol. 12, No. 1, 1990, pp. 13–21.

102 ANWAR, Muhammad, Review of *The Challenge of Islamic Economics* by Muhammad Akram Khan, in *The American Journal of Islamic Social Sciences*, Vol. 3, No. 2, 1986, pp. 231–4.

103 BARTHEL, Gunter, 'Islamic heritage and economy – in search of an assessment', *Asia, Africa, Latin America* (Berlin), No. 22, 1989, pp. 62–7.

104 BURKI, Shahid Javed, 'Economic management within an Islamic context', in Anita M. Weiss (ed.), *Islamic Reassertion in Pakistan*, Lahore: Vanguard, 1987, pp. 49–58.

105 CHAPRA, M. Umer, 'The need for a new economic system', *Review of Islamic Economics*, Vol. 1, 1991, pp. 9–47.

106 CHOUDHURY, Masudul Alam, 'The blending of religious and social orders in Islam', *International Journal of Social Economics*, Vol. 16, No. 2, 1989, pp. 13–45.

107 ENGINEER, Asghar Ali, *Islamic Approach to the Challenge of Poverty*, Occasional Papers No. 8, Vol. 6, Bombay: Institute of Islamic Studies, 1990.

108 EL-GHOWEIL, Ibrahim, 'The necessity for a new economic system', *Risalat al-Jihad* (Paola, Malta), no. 74, Autumn 1990, pp. 157–60.

109 HAMADANI, Viqar A., 'New Islamic economic order', *The Muslim World League Journal* (Makkah), October 1981, p. 29.

110 HAMDULAY, Jamaluddin Ahmed, *Islam: The Future Economic System*, Athlone, RSA: Bookworld Publishers, 1986.

111 HASSANI, Al-Hassani Bakir, *Iqtisad: The Islamic Alternative for Economics*, Lanham, MD: Imamia Centre, 1988.

112 AL-HOUDEBY, Samir, 'Muslims and the world of economics', *Risalat al-Jihad* (Paola, Malta), No. 74, Autumn 1990, pp. 142–52.

113 Islamic Council of Europe, *The Muslim World and the Future Economic Order*, London: Islamic Council of Europe, 1979.

114 IWAI, Satoshi, *A New Approach to Human Economics: A Case Study of an Islamic Economy*, Working Paper No. 2, Japan: Institute of Middle Eastern Studies, 1985, 111 pp.

115 JOMO, K.S. (ed.), *Islamic Economic Alternatives: Critical Perspectives and New Directions*, London: Macmillan, 1992, 180 pp.

116 KHAN, Ghulam Ishaq, 'Islamic economics reform as a vehicle of social change' (Inaugural address to a conference in Pakistan), *Journal of Islamic Banking and Finance* (Karachi), Vol. 6, No. 1, 1989, pp. 7–13.

117 KHAN, Muhammad Akram, *Fighting Rural Poverty: A Short-Term Strategy*, Lahore: All-Pakistan Islamic Education Congress 1991, 54 pp.

118 KHAN, Muhammad Akram, 'Elimination of poverty in the Islamic economic framework', *Islamic Studies* (Islamabad), Vol. 29, No. 2, 1990, pp. 143–62.

119 KHAN, Muhammad Akram, 'Islamic economics: the state of the art', in *Towards Islamization of Disciplines*, Herndon, VA: International Institute of Islamic Thought, 1989, pp. 273–92.

120 KHAN, M. Shabbir, *Islam: Social and Economic Structure*, New Delhi: Ashish Publication House, 1987, 147 pp.

121 KHAN, Mohsin S. and MIRAKHOR, Abbas, 'Islam and the economic system', *Review of Islamic Economics*, Vol. 2, No. 1, 1992, pp. 1–29.

122 KHARAFA, Ala-Eddin, 'Islamic economy', *The Muslim World League Journal* (Makkah), September 1982, p. 54.

123 KURAN, Timur, 'The economic system in contemporary Islamic thought: interpretation and assessment', *International Journal of Middle East Studies*, Vol. 18, 1986, pp. 135–64.

124 MANNAN, M.A., *The Frontiers of Islamic Economics*, Delhi: Idara-i-Adabiyat, 1984.

125 MANNAN, M.A., *Institutional Settings of Islamic Economic Order*, Jeddah: International Centre for Research in Islamic Economics, 1981.

126 MAUDOODI, S. Abul A'Ala, *The Economic Problem and Its Islamic Solution*, Lahore: Islamic Publications, 1978.

127 MIRAKHOR, Abbas, 'The economic system in an Islamic society', *Middle East Insight*, Vol. 5, No. 3, 1987, pp. 32–45.

128 MOLLA, R.I. (ed.), *Frontiers and Mechanics of Islamic Economics*, Sokoto, Nigeria: University of Sokoto, 1988.

129 NASR, Seyyed Vali Reza, 'Whither Islamic economics?', *Islamic Quarterly*, Vol. 30, No. 4, 1986, pp. 211–20.

130 National Bank of Pakistan, *Economic System of Islam: Proceedings of a Seminar*, Karachi: National Bank of Pakistan, 1980.

131 Pakistan, 'Report of the second international conference on Islamic economics', *Journal of Research in Islamic Economics*, Vol. 1, No. 2, 1983.

132 PARVIN, Manoucher, 'The political economy of divine unity: a critique of Islamic theory and practice', in Haleh Esfaudiari and A.L. Udovitch (eds.), *The Economic Dimensions of Middle Eastern History*, Princeton, NJ: Darwin Press, 1990, pp. 215–38.

133 PATEL, Z.A., *Small Kindness: Islamic Viewpoint on the Cause and Solution of Global Poverty*, Nuneaton: Muslim Venture Publications, 1990, 38 pp.

134 PHILIPP, T., 'The idea of Islamic economics', *Die Welt des Islams* (Leicester), Vol. 30, 1990, pp. 17–39.

135 RASHID, Salim, 'Islamic economics: a historico-inductive approach', *Journal of Islamic Banking and Finance* (Karachi), Vol. 6, No. 1, 1989, pp. 33–44.

136 RASHID, Salim, 'An agenda for Muslim economists: a historico-inductive approach', *Journal of King Abdul Aziz University: Islamic Economics* (Jeddah), Vol. 3, 1991, pp. 45–54.

137 SARDAR, Ziauddin, *Islamic Futures: The Shape of Ideas to Come*, London: Mansell, 1985.

138 SHAGHIL, M., *Islamic Economics: A Global Perspective*, New Delhi: Ashish Publishing House, 1989, 175 pp.

139 SHEIKH, Nasir A., *Some Aspects of the Constitution and the Economics of Islam*, Woking: Woking Mission, 1967.

140 SIDDIQI, M.N., 'An Islamic approach to economics', *Al-Tawhid* (Tehran), Vol. 4, No. 2, 1986–7, pp. 105–25.

141 SOULTAN, Lotfi Ali, 'The economic integration in Islam', *Al-Azhar Magazine* (Cairo), Vol. 62, No. 7, 1990, pp. 739–44.

142 UZAIR, Muhammad, 'An outline of interest-free economy – II', *The Muslim World League Journal* (Makkah), Vol. 14, No. 3, 1986, pp. 41–8.

143 ZAMAN, Hasanuz S.M., 'The objectives of economic policy in the early Islamic period', in *Economic System of Islam*, Karachi: National Bank of Pakistan, 1980, pp. 151–71.

Theory and Practice

144 ABDULLAH, Khalid and TARIQ, Al-Mansour, 'The impact of Islamic economics', *Arabia*, November 1984, p. 58.

145 ANSARI, Javed Akbar, 'The poverty of Islamic economics', *The Universal Message* (Karachi), Vol. 11, No. 9, 1990, pp. 7–10.

146 ANSARI, Javed Akbar, 'Pakistan's economic policy: an Islamic alternative to the fund and the bank', *The Universal Message* (Karachi), Vol. 12, No. 2, 1990, pp. 19–25.

147 ANSARI, Samad, 'Economic potential and integration of the Muslim world', *Journal of Islamic Banking and Finance* (Karachi), Vol. 7, No. 4, 1990, pp. 9–34.

148 BEHDAD, Sohrab, 'Winners and losers of the Iranian revolution: a study in income distribution', *International Journal of Middle East Studies*, Vol. 21, No. 3, 1989, pp. 327–58.

149 *Business Week*, 'A widening test of Islamic economics', *Business Week*, 17 March 1980, p. 161.

150 CHOUDHURY, Masudul Alam (ed.), *Islamic Economic Co-operation*, London: Macmillan, 1989, 472 pp.

151 CHOUDHURY, Masudul Alam, 'Contemporary Islamic economic thought', *Muslim Education Quarterly* (Cambridge), Vol. 8, No. 1, 1990, pp. 40–9.

152 HOSSEINI, Hamid, 'Islamic economics in Iran: is a new economic paradigm in the making?', *Journal of South Asian and Middle Eastern Studies* (Villanova, PA), Vol. 12, No. 2, 1988, pp. 21–44.

153 HOSSEINI, Hamid, 'From homo economicus to homo Islamicus: the universality of economic science reconsidered', in Cyrus Bina and Hamid Zangeneh, *Modern Capitalism and Islamic Ideology in Iran*, London: Macmillan, 1992, pp. 103–17.

154 'International seminar on Islamic economics and the economy of Indian Muslims' (New Delhi 21–24 July 1989), *Journal of Objective Studies* (Aligarh), Vol. 2, No. 1, 1990, pp. 127–37.

155 IONOVA, Alla, 'Illusions of the "Islamic economy"', *Asia and Africa Today*, No. 1, 1988, pp. 63–6.

156 'Islamic economics and the economy of Indian Muslims' (Conference report, 21–24 July 1989), *The American Journal of Islamic Social Sciences* (Herndon, VA), Vol. 6, No. 2, 1989, pp. 358–60.

157 KHAN, Abdul Jabbar, 'Elimination of beggary from Pakistan: some suggestions', *The Universal Message* (Karachi), Vol. 9, No. 9, 1988, pp. 26–7.

158 KHAN, M. Akram, *Challenge of Islamic Economics*, Lahore: All-Pakistan Islamic Education Congress, 1985.

159 KHAN, Muhammad Akram, 'The future of Islamic economics', *Futures*, April 1991, pp. 248–61.

160 MALIK, Azir A., 'Islamic economic co-operation in the South–South context', in Masudul Alam Choudhury (ed.), *Islamic Economic Co-operation*, London: Macmillan, 1989, pp. 375–410.

161 MANNAN, M.A., *The Making of Islamic Economic Society: Islamic Dimensions in Economic Analysis*, Cairo: International Association of Islamic Banks and Lefkosa: International Institute of Islamic Banking and Economics, 1984.

162 AL-MANSOUR, Khalid Abdullah Tariq, 'The impact of Islamic economics', *Arabia*, November 1984, pp. 58–9.

163 NAQVI, S.N.H., 'The margins of state intervention in an Islamic economy', *Hamdard Islamicus*, Autumn 1983, pp. 47–61.

164 NIENHAUS, Volker and CHOUDHURY, Masudul A., 'The potential impact of Islamic economic co-operation on the world economy', in Masudul Alam Choudhury (ed.), *Islamic Economic Co-operation*, London: Macmillan, 1989, pp. 352–74.

165 PAL, Izzud-Din, 'Pakistan, Islam and economics', *Journal of Contemporary Asia*, Vol. 17, No. 2, 1987, pp. 187–207.

166 'Recommendation of a three-day national seminar on fourth five-year plan organised by Islamic Economics Research Bureau, Dhaka, Bangladesh', Parts 1 and 2, *Al-Islam* (Dhaka), Vol. 6, No. 11, 1990, pp. 11–18 and No. 12, 1990, pp. 15–20.

167 'Second annual economics seminar', *The American Journal of Islamic Social Sciences* (Herndon, VA), Vol. 5, No. 2, 1988, pp. 317–18.

Political Economy of Islam

168 ALI, Ausaf, 'The political economy of the Islamic state: a comparative study', Ph.D. dissertation, University of Southern California, 1970.

169 AMIRA, Hamadi H., *Revolution and Economic Transition*, Albany, NY: State University of New York Press, 1990.

170 AMUZEGAR, Jahangir, 'The Iranian economy before and after the revolution', *Middle East Journal*, Vol. 46, No. 3, 1992, pp. 413–25.

171 AMUZEGAR, Jahangir, *Iran's economy under the Islamic Republic*, London: Tauris, 1993, 286 pp.

172 AZIZ, T.M., 'An Islamic perspective of political economy: the views of Martyr Muhammad Baqir-al-Sadr', *Al-Tawhid* (Tehran), Vol. 10, No. 1, 1992, pp. 139–54.

173 BEHDAD, Sohrab, 'The political economy of the Islamic planning in Iran', in H. Amirahmadi and M. Parvin (eds.), *Post-Revolutionary Iran*, Boulder, CO: Westview Press, 1988.

174 BINA, Cyrus and ZANGENEH, Hamid, *Modern Capitalism and Islamic Ideology in Iran*, London: Macmillan, 1992.

175 CHOUDHURY, Masudul Alam and MALIK, Uzie Abdul, *The Foundations of Islamic Political Economy*, New York: St Martin's Press, 1992, 260 pp.

176 CHOUDHURY, Masudul Alam, 'Toward organizing an Islamic political economy', *The Islamic Quarterly* (London), Vol. 36, No. 4, 1992, pp. 280–92.

177 EICKELMAN, Dale F., 'The political economy of religious culture: changing interpretation of Islamic movements', in William R. Roff (ed.), *Islam and the Political Economy of Meaning*, London: Croom Helm, 1987.

178 ENGINEER, Asghar Ali, 'Islamic economics: a progressive perspective', in K.S. Jomo (ed.), *Islamic Economic Alternatives*, London: Macmillan, 1992, pp. 117–24.

179 FARIDI, F.R., 'Islamisation of economics: the Indian and global context', *Journal of Objective Studies* (Aligarh), Vol. 2, No. 1, 1990, pp. 72–82.

180 GARDEZI, H.N., 'Islamization of economy in Pakistan (1977–88): an essay on the relationship between religion and economics: comment', *Pakistan Development Review*, Vol. 30, No. 4, 1991, pp. 1117–18.

181 GHASIMI, M., 'The Iranian economy after the revolution: an economic appraisal of the five-year plan', *International Journal of Middle Eastern Studies*, Vol. 24, No. 4, 1992, pp. 599–614.

182 GILANI, Ijaz Shafi, 'The political context of Islamic economics', in Khurshid Ahmad (ed.), *Studies in Islamic Economics*, Jeddah: International Institute of Research in Islamic Economics and Leicester: Islamic Foundation, 1980.

183 HABIBY, Raymond N., 'Mu'amar Qadhafi's new Islamic scientific Socialist Society', in M.S. Curtis (ed.), *The Middle East Reader*, Oxford: Transaction Books, 1986, pp. 225–32.

184 HAGHAYEGHI, Mehrdad, 'Agrarian reform problems in post-revolutionary Iran', *Middle Eastern Studies* (London), Vol. 26, No. 1, 1990, pp. 35–51.

185 HAQUE, Ziaul, 'Islamic perspective and class interest', in K.S. Jomo (ed.), *Islamic Economic Alternatives*, London: Macmillan, 1992, pp. 105–16.

186 HAQUE, Ziaul, 'Islamization of economy in Pakistan (1977–88): an essay on the relationship between religion and economics', *Pakistan Development Review*, Vol. 30, No. 4, 1991, pp. 1105–16.
187 HEFNER, Robert W., 'The political economy of Islamic conversion in modern East Java', in William R. Roff (ed.), *Islam and the Political Economy of Meaning*, London: Croom Helm, 1987.
188 HOSSEINI, H., 'From Buchanan to Khomeini: can neo-classical economics explain Iran's Islamic state?', *The American Journal of Economics and Sociology* (New York), Vol. 49, No. 2, 1990, pp. 167–84.
189 JALALUDDIN, Abul Khair Mohammad, *The Role of Government in an Islamic Economy*, Kuala Lumpur: Noordeen, 1991, 130 pp.
190 JAMES, William E. and ROY, Subroto (eds.), *Foundations of Pakistan's Political Economy: Towards an Agenda for the 1990s*, London: Sage, 1992, 301 pp.
191 KHAN, Omar Asghar, 'Economic aspects of Islamization in Pakistan', in K.S. Jomo (ed.), *Islamic Economic Alternatives*, London: Macmillan, 1992, pp. 139–52.
192 KHAN, Shahrukh Rafi, 'Political economy of an Islamic system', *Hamdard Islamicus*, No. 4, Winter 1985, pp. 3–34.
193 MANNAN, M.A. *et al.*, *International Economic Relations from Islamic Perspectives*, Jeddah: Islamic Research and Training Institute, Islamic Development Bank, 1992, 296 pp.
194 MARTY, Martin E. and APPLEBY, R. Scott (eds.), *Fundamentalism and the State: Remaking Politics, Economics and Militance*, Chicago: Chicago University Press, 1993, 665 pp.
195 MUSTAFA, N., 'On the renewal of interest in international political economy', *Maj al-Ulum al-Ijtima'iya*, Vol. 14, No. 3, 1986, pp. 14–42.
196 NAQVI, Syed Nawab Haider *et al.*, 'Principles of Islamic economic reform', in K.S. Jomo (ed.), *Islamic Economic Alternatives*, London: Macmillan, 1992, pp. 153–87.
197 ROFF, William R. (ed.), *Islam and the Political Economy of Meaning*, London: Croom Helm, 1987.
198 YUGHMAIAN, Behzad, 'Recent development in the political economy of Iran', in Cyrus Bina and Hamid Zangeneh, *Modern Capitalism and Islamic Ideology in Iran*, London: Macmillan, 1992, pp. 159–88.

4

ISLAMIC ECONOMIC THEORIES

General

199 ABU SULAIMAN, A. Hamid, 'The theory of the economics of Islam', in Muslim Students Association of the United States and Canada, *Contemporary Aspects of Economic Thinking in Islam*, Bloomington, IN: MSA, 1976.

200 AHMAD, Ehsan, 'Modelling interest-free economy' (Review article), *The American Journal of Islamic Social Sciences*, Vol. 7, No. 1, 1990, pp. 111–12.

201 AHMAD, Khurshid (ed.), *Studies in Islamic Economics*, Leicester: Islamic Foundation, 1980, 173 pp.

202 AHMAD, Salahuddin (ed.), *Thoughts on Economics*, Special issue of the Conference on Distribution of Income and Wealth in Islam, Dhaka: Islamic Economics Research Bureau, 1989, 142 pp.

203 AKKAS, S.M. Ali, 'Size distribution of income and wealth in an Islamic economic framework', *Thoughts on Economics* (Dhaka), Vol. 8, No. 3–4, 1987, pp. 68–75.

204 BENDJILALI, Boualem, 'On Muslim consumer behaviour: a mathematical set-up', *Journal of Islamic Economics*, Vol. 3, No. 1, 1993, pp. 1–16.

205 BENDJILALI, B. and BACHIR, F., 'Towards a theory of the behaviour of the Muslim consumer', *Journal of Social Sciences* (Kuwait), 1985, 1989.

206 BIRAIMA, M.E., 'A Qur'anic model for a universal economic theory', *Journal of King Abdul Aziz University: Islamic Economics* (Jeddah), Vol. 3, 1991, pp. 3–41.

207 CHAPRA, M. Umer, *Islam and the Economic Challenge*, Leicester: Islamic Foundation and International Institute of Islamic Thought, 1992, 428 pp.

208 CHISHTI, Salim U., 'Relative stability of interest-free economy', *Journal of Research in Islamic Economics*, Vol. 3, No. 1, 1985, pp. 3–12.

209 CHOUDHURY, Masudul Alam, 'Principles of Islamic economics', *Middle Eastern Studies*, January 1983, pp. 93–104.

210 CHOUDHURY, Masudul Alam, *Contributions to Islamic Economic Theory*, New York: Macmillan, 1986.

211 CHOUDHURY, Masudul Alam, 'The blending of religious and social orders in the Islamic economic order', *International Journal of Social Economics*, No. 4, 1986, pp. 60–70.

212 CHOUDHURY, Masudul Alam, *Islamic Economic Co-operation*, London: Macmillan, 1989.

213 CHOUDHURY, Masudul Alam, *Contribution to Islamic Economic Theory: A Study in Social Economics*, London: Macmillan, 1986, 291 pp.

214 CHOUDHURY, Masudul Alam, 'The humanomic structure of Islamic economic theory', *Journal of King Abdul Aziz University: Islamic Economics* (Jeddah), Vol. 2, 1990, pp. 47–64.

215 FARIDI, F.R. (ed.), *Aspects of Islamic Economics and the Economy of Indian Muslims*, New Delhi: Genuine Publications and Media, 1993.

216 GHANAMEH, Abdul Hadi, 'The interest-less economy', in Muslim Students Association of the United States and Canada, *Contemporary Aspects of Economic and Social Thinking in Islam*, Gary, IN: MSA, 1973.

217 HAQUE, Ziaul, Review of *Studies in Islamic Economics* ed. by Khurshid Ahmad, in *Hamdard Islamicus*, Vol. 5, No. 1, 1982.

218 HAQUE, Ziaul, *Islam and Feudalism*, Lahore: Vanguard, 1984.

219 HUSAIN, Muzaffar, *Motivation for Economic Achievement in Islam*, Lahore: All-Pakistan Educational Congress, 1974.

220 KAHF, Monzer, 'Islamic economic system review', *Al-Ittihad*, January 1978, pp. 41–52.

221 KHAN, M. Akram, *Issues in Islamic Economics*, Lahore: Islamic Publications, 1983.

222 KHAN, M. Akram, 'Resource allocation in an Islamic economy', *Islamic Quarterly*, Vol. 29, No. 4, 1985.

223 KHAN, Muhammad Fayyaz (ed.), *Islamic Economy: A Matter of Interest*, Special issue of *The Message International*, Vol. 16, No. 7, 1992, Jamaica, NY: Message International, 1992, 46 pp.

224 MANNAN, M.A., *Islamic Economics: Theory and Practice*, London: Hodder and Stoughton, 1986, 432 pp.

225 MANNAN, M.A., *The Making of Islamic Economic Society: Islamic Dimensions in Economic Analysis*, Cairo: International Association of Islamic Banks, 1984.
226 MANNAN, M.A., *Economic Development and Social Peace in Islam*, London: Ta-Ha Publishers, 1989.
227 MIRAKHOR, Abbas and ZAIDI, Iqbal, 'Stabilization and growth in an open Islamic economy', in A. Ahmad and K.R. Awan (eds.), *Lectures on Islamic Economics*, Jeddah: Islamic Development Bank, 1992, pp. 395–419.
228 PEERZADE, Syed Afzal, 'The idea of merit effect: Islam's contribution to economics', *Journal of Objective Studies* (Aligarh), Vol. 3, No. 1, 1991, pp. 1–22.
229 POWERS, D.S., 'The Islamic inheritance system: a socio-historical approach', *Arab Law Quarterly*, Vol. 8, No. 1, 1993, pp. 13–29.
230 ROSENTHAL, F., *Gambling in Islam*, Leiden: Brill, 1975.
231 SIDDIQI, Muhammad Nejatullah, 'Role of the voluntary sector in Islam: a conceptual framework', *Al Tawhid* (Tehran), Vol. 5, No. 2, 1987–8, pp. 131–55.
232 SIDDIQI, M.N., *The Economic Enterprise in Islam*, Lahore: Islamic publications.
233 SIDDIQUI, Muhammad Yasin Mazhar, 'Economic imbalances and the role of Islam – an essay in Quranic interpretation', *Hamdard Islamicus*, Vol. 10, No. 2, 1987, pp. 35–46.
234 'Ten suggestions for building an interest-free economy', *Al-Farooq International* (Karachi), Vol. 3, No. 10, 1991, pp. 12–17.
235 'The irresistible surge from the Muslim South: a study of economic imbalances', *The Muslim World League Journal* (Makkah al-Mukarramah), Vol. 19, No. 5, 1991, p. 48.
236 UZAIR, M., 'Foreign trade in an interest-less economy', *Voices of Islam* (Karachi), Vol. 7, No. 2–3, pp. 96–103.
237 ZAMAN, M. Raquibuz, 'Business organization and the investments for raising financial capital for a modern Islamic economy', *Islamic Culture* (Hyderabad), Vol. 60, No. 3, 1986, pp. 1–20.
238 ZARQA, Muhammad Anas, 'A partial relationship in a Muslim's utility function', in S. Tahir *et al.* (eds.), *Readings in Microeconomics: An Islamic Perspective*, Petaling Jaya: Longman Malaysia, 1992, pp. 105–12.

Micro-Models of Islamic Economics

239 AGIL, Syed Omar Syed, 'Rationality in economic theory', in S. Tahir *et al.* (eds.), *Readings in Microeconomics: An Islamic Perspective*, Petaling Jaya: Longman Malaysia, 1992, pp. 31–48.

240 AHMAD, Salahuddin, 'Pattern of consumption and saving behaviour in an Islamic economy', *Thoughts on Economics*, Vol. 7, No. 1, 1986, pp. 1–38.

241 ARIFF, Mohammad, 'Towards establishing the microfoundations of Islamic economics', *Islamic Quarterly*, Vol. 28, No. 2, pp. 61–72.

242 EL-ASHKER, Ahmed A., *On the Islamic Theory of Economic Behaviour: An Empirical Enquiry in a Non-Islamic Country*, Durham: Centre for Middle Eastern and Islamic Studies, University of Durham, 1986, 18 pp.

243 BENDJILALI, Boualem and TAHER, Farid B., 'A zero efficiency loss monopolist: an Islamic perspective', *The American Journal of Islamic Social Sciences* (Herndon, VA), Vol. 7, No. 2, 1990, pp. 219–32.

244 CHOUDHURY, M.A., 'Micro-economic foundation of Islamic economics', *The American Journal of Islamic Social Sciences* (Herndon, VA), Vol. 2, 1986, pp. 231–45.

245 CHOUDHURY, Masudul A., 'Social choice in an Islamic economic framework', *The American Journal of Islamic Social Sciences* (Herndon, VA). Vol. 8, No. 2, 1991, pp. 259–74.

246 ELGARI, M.A., 'Some Islamic insights on the theory of consumer behaviour', *Journal of Objective Studies* (Aligarh), Vol. 1, 1990, pp. 1–9.

247 HABIBULLAH, M., 'Management in the eye of Islam', *Thoughts on Economics*, Vol. 7, No. 2, 1986, pp. 21–30.

248 HAMOURI, Qasem, 'Rationality, time and accounting for the future in Islamic thought', in F.R. Faridi (ed.), *Essays in Islamic Economic Analysis*, New Delhi: Genuine Publications and Media, 1991, pp. 67–81.

249 HASAN, Zubair, 'Profit-maximization: secular versus Islamic', in S. Tahir *et al.* (eds.), *Readings in Microeconomics: An Islamic Perspective*, Petaling Jaya: Longman Malaysia, 1992, pp. 239–55.

250 HUSSAIN, M. Sharif, 'Concept of factors of production and their remuneration in the Islamic perspective', *Thoughts on Economics* (Dhaka), Vol. 8, No. 3–4, 1987, pp. 107–18.

251 IQBAL, Munawar, 'Organization of production and theory of firm behaviour from an Islamic perspective', in A. Ahmad and

K.R. Awan (eds.), *Lectures on Islamic Economics*, Jeddah: Islamic Development Bank, 1992, pp. 205–16.

252 ISHAQUE, Khalid M., 'Islamic principles of economic management', *Al-'Ilm*, Vol. 6, January 1986, pp. 26–50.

253 ISHAQUE, Khalid M., 'Islamic principles of economic management', *Al-'Ilm*, Vol. 7, January 1987, pp. 14–49.

254 ISLAM, M. Zohurul, 'An Islamic approach to distribution of income among the participating factors in the framework of Islam', *Thoughts on Economics* (Dhaka), Vol. 8, No. 3–4, 1987, pp. 59–67.

255 ISLAM, Tariq Saiful, 'Productivity measurement: a discussion of two crucial issues', *Thoughts on Economics* (Dhaka), Vol. 7, No. 3, 1986, pp. 10–13.

256 AL-JUNID, Syed Abdul Hamid, 'Factors of production and factor pricing from an Islamic perspective', in S. Tahir *et al.* (eds.), *Readings in Microeconomics: An Islamic Perspective*, Petaling Jaya: Longman Malaysia, 1992, pp. 256–71.

257 KAHF, Monzer, 'Market structure: free co-operation', in S. Tahir *et al.* (eds.), *Readings in Microeconomics: An Islamic Perspective*, Petaling Jaya: Longman Malaysia, 1992, pp. 146–56.

258 KAHF, Monzer, 'Theory of consumptions', in S. Tahir *et al.* (eds.), *Readings in Microeconomics: An Islamic Perspective*, Petaling Jaya: Longman Malaysia, 1992, pp. 61–8.

259 KAHF, Monzer, 'A contribution to the theory of consumer behaviour in an Islamic society', in S. Tahir *et al.* (eds.), *Readings in Microeconomics: An Islamic Perspective*, Petaling Jaya: Longman Malaysia, 1992, pp. 90–104.

260 KAHF, Monzer, 'The theory of production', in S. Tahir *et al.* (eds.), *Readings in Microeconomics: An Islamic Perspective*, Petaling Jaya: Longman Malaysia, 1992, pp. 113–19.

261 KHAN, Muhammad Akram, 'Resource allocation in an Islamic economy', in S. Tahir *et al.* (eds.), *Readings in Microeconomics: An Islamic Perspective*, Petaling Jaya: Longman Malaysia, 1992, pp. 184–92.

262 KHAN, Mohammad Fahim, 'Theory of consumer behaviour in an Islamic perspective', in S. Tahir *et al.* (eds.), *Readings in Microeconomics: An Islamic Perspective*, Petaling Jaya: Longman Malaysia, 1992, pp. 69–80.

263 KHAN, Mohammad Fahim, 'Factors of production and factor markets in Islamic framework', *Journal of King Abdul Aziz University: Islamic Economics* (Jeddah), Vol. 2, 1990, pp. 25–45.

264 KHAN, Mohammad Fahim and GIFARI, Noor Muhammed, 'Al-Shatibi's objectives of Shariah and some implications for consumer theory' (12th-century jurist), in A.H.M. Sadeq and A. Ghazali (eds.), *Readings in Islamic Economic Thought*, Petaling Jaya: Longman Malaysia, 1992, pp. 176–202.

265 KURAN, T., 'Behavioural norms in the Islamic doctrines of economics – a critique', *Journal of Economic Behaviour and Organization*, 1983.

266 MANNAN, M.A., 'Islamic perspectives on market prices and allocation', in S. Tahir *et al.* (eds.), *Readings in Microeconomics: An Islamic Perspective*, Petaling Jaya: Longman Malaysia, 1992, pp. 193–219.

267 MANNAN, M.A., 'The behaviour of the firm and its objectives in an Islamic framework', in S. Tahir *et al.* (eds.), *Readings in Microeconomics: An Islamic Perspective*, Petaling Jaya: Longman Malaysia, 1992, pp. 120–30.

268 MANNAN, M.A., 'Islamic perspectives on market imperfections with special reference to the theory of monopoly', in S. Tahir *et al.* (eds.), *Readings in Microeconomics: An Islamic Perspective*, Petaling Jaya: Longman Malaysia, 1992, pp. 176–83.

269 MANNAN, M.A., *Islamic Perspectives on Market Prices and Allocation*, Jeddah: International Centre for Research in Islamic Economics, 1982.

270 METWALLY, M.M., 'A behavioural model of an Islamic firm', in S. Tahir *et al.* (eds.), *Readings in Microeconomics: An Islamic Perspective*, Petaling Jaya: Longman Malaysia, 1992, pp. 131–38.

271 RASHID, Salim, 'Project evaluation in an Islamic framework', *Journal of Islamic Banking and Finance*, October–December 1987, pp. 61–9.

272 RUSHDI, Ali Ahmed, 'Monopoly in Islam: a case for cross subsidization', *Thoughts on Economics*, Vol. 8, No. 1, 1987, pp. 38–62.

273 SADEQ, Abul Hasan M., 'Factor pricing and income distribution from an Islamic perspective', in S. Tahir *et al.* (eds.), *Readings in Microeconomics: An Islamic Perspective*, Petaling Jaya: Longman Malaysia, 1992, pp. 272–86.

274 SIDDIQI, M.N., 'Islamic consumer behaviour', in S. Tahir *et al.* (eds.), *Readings in Microeconomics: An Islamic Perspective*, Petaling Jaya: Longman Malaysia, 1992, pp. 49–60.

275 SIDDIQI, M.N., 'Islamic producer behaviour', in S. Tahir *et al.* (eds.), *Readings in Microeconomics: An Islamic Perspective*, Petaling Jaya: Longman Malaysia, 1992, pp. 139–45.

276 SIDDIQI, M.N., 'Monopoly and monopolistic competition', in S. Tahir *et al.* (eds.), *Readings in Microeconomics: An Islamic Perspective*, Petaling Jaya: Longman Malaysia, 1992, pp. 165–75.
277 TAHIR, Sayyid *et al.* (eds.), *Readings in Microeconomics: An Islamic Perspective*, Petaling Jaya: Longman Malaysia, 1992, 298 pp.
278 ZAMAN, Asad, 'Towards foundations for an Islamic theory of consumer', in S. Tahir *et al.* (eds.), *Readings in Microeconomics: An Islamic Perspective*, Petaling Jaya: Longman Malaysia, 1992, pp. 81–9.

Macro-Models of Islamic Economics

279 AHMAD, Abu, 'A macro framework for an interest-free economy', in M.A. Huq (ed.), *Thoughts on Islamic Banking*, Dhaka: Islamic Economics Research Bureau, 1982, pp. 160–63.
280 AHMAD, Ausaf, 'A macro model of distribution in Islamic economy', *Journal of Research in Islamic Economics*, Vol. 2, No. 1, 1984, pp. 1–20.
281 AHMAD, Ausaf, 'Macroconsumption function in an Islamic framework: a survey of current literature', in A. Ahmad and K.R. Awan (eds.), *Lectures on Islamic Economics*, Jeddah: Islamic Development Bank, 1992, pp. 245–76.
282 ANWAR, Muhammad, 'A macroeconomic model for interest-free economies: an integrative study of Western and Islamic economic systems', Ph.D. dissertation, University of New Hampshire.
283 AZHAR, Rauf Ahmed, 'A theory of optimal investment decision in an Islamic economy', in A. Ahmad and K.R. Awan (eds.), *Lectures on Islamic Economics*, Jeddah: Islamic Development Bank, 1992, pp. 217–43.
284 BEHDAD, Sohrab, 'Islamic economics: a utopian–scholastic–neoclassical–Keynesian synthesis', *Research in the History of Economic Thought and Methodology*, Vol. 7, 1991.
285 CHOUDHURY, Masudul Alam and RAHMAN, A.N.M. Azizur, 'Macroeconomic relations in the Islamic economic order', *International Journal of Social Economics*, Vol. 13, No. 4, 1986, pp. 60–70.
286 FARIDI, F.R., *Essays in Islamic Economic Analysis*, New Delhi: Qazi Publishers and Distributors, 1991.
287 AL-FARUQI, Maysami, 'Studies in the theory of value: a critical analysis of classical, neo-classical and post-Keynesian theories

and elaboration of Islamic theory', Ph.D. dissertation, Temple University, 1989, 337 pp.

288 UL-HAQUE, Nadeem and MIRAKHOR, Abbas, 'Saving behaviour in an economy without fixed interest', *Journal of Islamic Banking and Finance* (Karachi), Vol. 6, No. 3, 1989, pp. 24–38.

289 HASSANEIN, Medhet, 'Towards a model of the economics of Islam', in *Contemporary Aspects of Economic Thinking in Islam*, Indianapolis: American Trust Publications, 1980.

290 KAHF, Monzer, *The Islamic Economy: Analytical Study of the Functioning of the Islamic Economic System*, Muslim Students Association of the United States and Canada, American Trust Publications, 1978.

291 KAHF, Monzer, 'Saving and investment functions in a two-sector Islamic economy', in A.H.M. Sadeq (ed.), *Financing Economic Development: Islamic and Mainstream Approaches*, Petaling Jaya: Longman Malaysia, 1992, pp. 36–55.

292 KHAN, M. Fahim, 'Macro consumption function in an Islamic framework', *Journal of Research in Islamic Economics*, Winter 1984, pp. 1–24. See also the comments on this article by Seif E.I. Tagel-Din in the Summer 1985 issue of this journal, pp. 57–61, and by S. Iqbal Mahdi and Zubair Hasan in the Winter 1985 issue, pp. 73–7 and 79–81.

293 KHAN, M. Fahim, *Distribution in Macroeconomic Framework: An Islamic Perspective*, Islamabad: International Institute of Islamic Economics, International Islamic University, 1989, pp. 111–44.

294 MAHDI, Syed Iqbal, 'Islamic approach to model building in economics and other social sciences: a methodological framework', *Journal of Objective Studies* (Aligarh), Vol. 1, 1990, pp. 83–94.

295 MAHDI, Syed Iqbal, 'Consumption function in Islamic economics', *The American Journal of Islamic Studies*, Vol. 1, August 1984, pp. 133–6.

296 MAHDI, Syed Iqbal and AL-ASALY, Saif, 'A model of income determination in an interest-free Islamic economy', in F.R. Faridi (ed.), *Essays in Islamic Economic Analysis*, New Delhi: Genuine Publications and Media, 1991, pp. 52–66.

297 MANNAN, M.A., 'Allocative efficiency, decision and welfare in criteria in an interest-free Islamic economy: a comparative policy approach', in Mohammad Ariff (ed.), *Monetary and Fiscal Economics of Islam*, Jeddah: International Centre for Research in Islamic Economics, King Abdul Aziz University, 1982, pp. 43–74.

298 METWALLY, M.M., *Macro-Economic Models of Islamic Doctrines*, London: JK Publishers, 1981.
299 SIDDIQUI, S.A. and ZAMAN, A., 'Investment and income distribution pattern under Musharaka finance: the certainty case', *Pakistan Journal of Applied Economics*, Vol. 8, No. 1, 1989, pp. 1–30.
300 TAHIR, Syed, 'A contribution to the theory of determination of aggregate output, income and economic inequalities in an Islamic economy', in A. Ahmad and K.R. Awan (eds.), *Lectures on Islamic Economics*, Jeddah: Islamic Development Bank, 1992, pp. 289–320.
301 TEKIR, Sabir, 'Modelling interest-free economy: a study in macro-economics and development', *The American Journal of Islamic Social Sciences* (Herndon, VA), Vol. 6, No. 2, 1989, pp. 373–5.
302 TOUTOUNCHIAN, I., 'Consumer durables, investment and financial cooperatives in the Islamic framework', Ph.D. dissertation, Texas A and M University, 1977.
303 ULGENER, Sabri F., 'Monetary conditions of economic growth and the Islamic concept of interest', *Islamic Review* (London), Vol. 55, No. 2, 1967, pp. 11–14.
304 ZAIDI, Iqbal and MIRAKHOR, Abbas, 'Stabilization and growth in an open Islamic economy', *Review of Islamic Economics* (Leicester), Vol. 1, No. 2, 1991, pp. 1–20.
305 ZARQA, M. Anas, 'Stability in an interest-free Islamic economy: a note', *Pakistan Journal of Applied Economics*, Winter 1983, pp. 181–8.
306 ZARQA, M. Anas, 'Capital allocation, efficiency and growth in an interest-free Islamic economy', *Journal of Economics and Administration* (Jeddah), November 1982, pp. 43–55.

5

ECONOMIC DEVELOPMENT AND GROWTH IN ISLAM

Concepts and approaches

307 AHMAD, Khurshid, 'Economic development in an Islamic framework', in K. Ahmad (ed.), *Studies in Islamic Economics*, Leicester: Islamic Foundation, 1980, pp. 171–88.

308 ALGABID, Hamid, *Islam and Development* (Seminar paper), Niamey: Organization of the Islamic Conference, 1992.

309 ALHABSHI, S. Othman, 'The role of ethics in economics and business', in A.H.M. Sadeq *et al.* (eds.), *Development and Finance in Islam*, Selangor: International Islamic University Press, 1991, pp. 41–54.

310 AWAD, A. Safi El-Din, 'Othman A. Llewellyn, "Islamic jurisprudence and environmental planning"' (Comments), *Journal of Research in Islamic Economics*, Vol. 3, No. 1, 1985, pp. 83–6.

311 BADAWI, Jamal, 'Concept of development from Islamic perspective', *Al-Nahdah* (Kuala Lumpur), Vol. 9, No. 1, 1989, pp. 20–4.

312 CHOUDHURY, M.A., 'The concept of Islamic socio-economic development in contemporary perspectives', *The Journal of Development Studies*, 1990, pp. 1–10.

313 DEEN, Mawil Y. Izzi, 'Islamic environmental ethics: law and society', in J. Ronald Engel and Joan Gibb Engel (eds.), *Ethics of Environment and Development*, Tucson, AZ: University of Arizona Press, 1990, pp. 189–200.

314 DURAN, Khalid, 'Islam and socio-economic development: reflections inspired by Mohammed Talibi', in L. Swindler (ed.), *Muslims in Dialogue*, Lampeter: Edwin Mellen Press, 1992, pp. 155–67.

315 ENGINEER, Asghar Ali, *The Origin and Development of Islam: An Essay on Its Socio-Economic Growth*, Bombay: Longman, 1980.

316 FUJUN, Jiao, 'Religion and economic development', *Third Concept* (New Delhi), Vol. 7, No. 77, July 1993, pp. 19–21.

317 HUSAINI, Waqar Ahmed, *An Islamic Assessment of Development and Belligerence in the Sub-Himalay Countries: Policy Implications for India, Pakistan, Bangladesh, USA and Global Development Planning*, International Studies Working Papers, Stanford, CA: Hoover Institution, 1991, 108 pp.

318 ISHAQUE, K.M., *The Islamic Approach to Economic Activity and Development*, London: Islamic Council of Europe, 1979, pp. 74–100.

318a LLEWELLYN, Othman A., 'Islamic jurisprudence and environmental planning' (Rejoinder to the comments of A. Safi El-Din Awad), *Journal of Research in Islamic Economics*, Vol. 3, No. 1, 1985, pp. 87–92.

319 MANNAN, M.A., *Economic Development and Social Peace in Islam*, London: Ta-Ha Publishers, 1989, 126 pp.

320 EL-MANOUFI, Kamal, 'Islam and development: a field study', in Tawfiq E. Farah and Y. Kuroda (eds.), *Political Socialization in the Arab States*, Boulder, CO: Lynne Rienner, 1987, pp. 147–57.

321 MEHMET, Ozay, 'Islam and development' (Forum), *Prisma: The Indonesian Indicator*, No. 42, December 1986, pp. 104–8.

322 MEHMET, Ozay, *Islamic Identity and Development: Studies of the Islamic Periphery*, London: Routledge, 1990, 272 pp.

323 MILES, William F.S., 'Islam and development in the Western Sahel: engine or brake?', *Journal Institute of Muslim Minority Affairs*, Vol. 7, No. 2, July 1986, pp. 439–63.

324 AL-MUTAIRI, Hezam M., 'An Islamic perspective towards development', *Hamdard Islamicus*, Vol. 16, No. 4, 1993, pp. 27–50.

325 AL-NAJJAR, Ahmad, 'The healthy path towards economic development: the Islamic alternative', Paper presented at the International Seminar on Islamic Social Justice, Ahmadu Bello University, Nigeria, 3–8 January 1978.

326 No entry.

327 POINGAN, Guimba B., 'Islam and development', *Islamic Herald*, Vol. 11, No. 1, 1987, pp. 7–13.

328 PRAMANIK, Ataul Huq, *Economic Development and Distribution in Islam*, London: Grey Seal Books, 1991, 256 pp.

329 SADEQ, A.H.M., *Economic Development in Islam*, Selangor: Pelanduk, 1990.

330 SALLEH, Muhammad Syukri, *An Islamic Approach to Rural Development – The Arqam Way* (Malaysia), London: ASOIB International, 1992, 326 pp.

331 SHARIF, M. Raihan, *The Concept of Economic Development in Islam*, Dhaka: Islamic Economics Research Bureau, 1986, 23 pp.

332 WASEEM, S.M., 'Development policy of the Islamic Republic of Iran', *Journal of the West Asian Studies Society* (Aligarh), No. 2, 1986, pp. 61–72.

333 ZARABOZO, 'A basic need approach is the Islamic approach to development', *Al-Ittihad*, October–December 1980.

Mobilization of Resources

334 ARIFF, Mohammad, 'Resource mobilization through the Islamic voluntary sector', in M. Ariff (ed.), *The Islamic Voluntary Sector in Southeast Asia*, Pasir Panjang, Singapore: Institute of Southeast Asian Studies, 1991, pp. 31–49.

335 AZIZ, A., 'Firm level decision and human resource development in an Islamic economy', *The American Journal of Islamic Social Sciences*, Vol. 10, No. 2, 1993, pp. 210–16.

336 CHAPRA, M. Umer, 'Economic development in Muslim countries: a strategy for development in the light of Islamic teachings', Paper presented at the Seminar on Islamic Economics, Cairo, 6–9 September 1988, held under the auspices of the International Institute of Islamic Thought, Washington, DC, and the Al-Azhar University, Cairo.

337 DUTTON, Yassin, 'Natural resources in Islam', in F. Khalid (ed.), *Islam and Ecology*, London: Cassell, 1992, pp. 51–67.

338 HANIFF, Ghulam M., 'Muslim development at risk: the crisis of human resources', *The American Journal of Islamic Social Sciences*, Vol. 9, No. 4, 1992, pp. 514–32.

339 IQBAL, Munawar, 'Financing economic development', in A.H.M. Sadeq *et al.* (eds.), *Development and Finance in Islam*, Selangor: International Islamic University Press, 1991, pp. 101–28.

340 ISLAM, M. Zohurul, 'Towards an economic development model in an Islamic economy', *Thoughts on Economics*, Vol. 7, No. 2, 1986, pp. 31–41.

341 KHAN, M. Fahim, *Resource Mobilization through the Profit–Loss Sharing Based Financial System*, Jeddah: Islamic Research and Training Institute, Islamic Development Bank, 1992.

342 MAHDAVY, H., 'The patterns and problems of economic development in rentier states: the case of Iran', in M.A. Cook (ed.), *Studies in the Economic History of the Middle East: From the*

Rise of Islam to the Present Day, London: Oxford University Press, 1970.

343 SADEQ, Abul Hasan M., 'Development and development finance in Islam', in A.H.M. Sadeq (ed.), *Financing Economic Development: Islamic and Mainstream Approaches*, Petaling Jaya: Longman Malaysia, 1992, pp. 1–7.

344 SADEQ, Abul Hasan M., 'Resource mobilization for development', in A.H.M. Sadeq (ed.), *Financing Economic Development: Islamic and Mainstream Approaches*, Petaling Jaya: Longman Malaysia, 1992, pp. 81–95.

345 SADEQ, Abul Hasan M., 'Development finance in an Islamic economy: external sources', in A.H.M. Sadeq (ed.), *Financing Economic Development: Islamic and Mainstream Approaches*, Petaling Jaya: Longman Malaysia, 1992, pp. 25–35.

346 SADEQ, Abul Hasan M., 'Development finance in an Islamic economy: domestic sources', in A.H.M. Sadeq (ed.), *Financing Economic Development: Islamic and Mainstream Approaches*, Petaling Jaya: Longman Malaysia, 1992, pp. 11–24.

347 SADEQ, Abul Hasan M., 'Economic growth in an Islamic economy', in A.H.M. Sadeq *et al.* (eds.), *Development and Finance in Islam*, Selangor: International Islamic University Press, 1991, pp. 55–72.

348 SADEQ, Abul Hasan M. (ed.), *Financing Economic Development: Islamic and Mainstream Approaches*, Petaling Jaya: Longman Malaysia, 1992, 239 pp.

349 SADEQ, A.H.M., 'Mobilization of resources for development', *The American Journal of Islamic Social Sciences* (Herndon, VA), Vol. 6, No. 2, 1989, pp. 239–56.

350 SATTAR, Zaidi, 'Report on the third seminar on Islamic economics: resource mobilization and investment in an Islamic framework' (Held at the Catholic University of America, Washington, DC, 22–23 December 1990), *The American Journal of Islamic Social Sciences* (Herndon, VA), Vol. 8, No. 1, 1991, pp. 181–9.

351 SHAIKH, Abdul Quader J., 'The feasibility of applying the US minority business development model to stimulate entrepreneurship among Indian Muslims', *Journal of Objective Studies* (Aligarh), Vol. 1, No. 1–2, 1989, pp. 1–11.

352 THIRLWALL, A.P., 'Financing economic development from domestic sources', in A.H.M. Sadeq (ed.), *Financing Economic Development: Islamic and Mainstream Approaches*, Petaling Jaya: Longman Malaysia, 1992, pp. 169–200.

353 THIRLWALL, A.P., 'The finance of development from external sources', in A.H.M. Sadeq (ed.), *Financing Economic Development: Islamic and Mainstream Approaches*, Petaling Jaya: Longman Malaysia, 1992, pp. 201–26.

Problems and Issues

354 ABECASSIS, David, *Identity, Islam and Human Development in Rural Bangladesh*, Dhaka: University Press, 1990.

355 AHMAD, Salahuddin (ed.), *Dimensions of Development in Islam*, Dhaka: Islamic Economics Research Bureau, 1991.

356 ALI, Ahmad, 'Economic problems of Muslim minorities: the case of Fiji Muslims', *Journal Institute of Muslim Minority Affairs*, Vol. 9, No. 1–2, 1982, pp. 82–103.

357 AMIJI, Hatim M., 'Islam and socio-economic development: case study of a Muslim minority in Tanzania', *Journal Institute of Muslim Minority Affairs*, Vol. 4, No. 1–2, 1982, p. 175.

358 ASKARI, Hasan, 'Religion and development: search for conceptual clarity and new methodology – the special case of Islam', *Islamic Quarterly*, Vol. 30, No. 2, 1986, pp. 75–81.

359 HANIFF, Ghulam M., 'The human resources path to development: a challenge to Muslims', *Islamic Studies*, Summer 1990, pp. 131–42.

360 KHAN, M. Azam, *Economics and Politics of Development: An Islamic Perspective*, Karachi: Royal Book Co., 1988, 228 pp.

360a SUTCLIFFE, C.R., 'Is Islam an obstacle to development?', *The Journal of Developing Areas*, October 1975, pp. 77–81.

6

ISLAMIC CONCEPT OF THE WELFARE STATE

Role of the Islamic State

361 ANSARI, Mohammad I., 'A critique of an interdependent welfare function in an Islamic society', *Humanomics*, Vol. 7, No. 2, 1991.

362 AZMI, S.H., 'Traditional Islamic social welfare: its meaning, history and contemporary relevance', Part 2, *The Islamic Quarterly* (London), Vol. 35, No. 4, 1991, pp. 209–24.

363 CHAPRA, M. Umer, 'The Islamic welfare state and its role in the economy', in Khurshid Ahmad (ed.), *Studies in Islamic Economics*, Leicester: Islamic Foundation, for the International Centre for Research in Islamic Economics, King Abdul Aziz University, Jeddah, 1980, pp. 143–69.

364 CHOUDHURY, Masudul Alam, 'Concept of time in Islamic social welfare function', *Journal of Objective Studies* (Aligarh), Vol. 3, No. 2, 1991, pp. 1–21.

365 HANNAN, Janab Shah Abdul, *The Role of the Government in an Islamic Economy*, Research Monograph Series No. 3, Dhaka: Islamic Economics Research Bureau, 1991, 20 pp.

366 KABBARA, A., 'The Islamic state and economic intervention', *Arab Banker*, Vol. 6, No. 6, 1986, pp. 26–31.

367 AL-KAFF, S.H.A.R., 'Financing a modern Islamic welfare state', *Radiance Views Weekly* (Delhi), Vol. 26, No. 12, 1990, pp. 6–7, 10.

368 QUDDUS, Syed Abdul, *Pakistan: Towards a Welfare State*, Karachi: Royal Book Co., 1989, 300 pp.

369 SAKR, M.A., 'The role of the state in the economic system of Islam', in *Islam and a New International Economic Order: The Social Dimension*, Geneva: IILS, 1980, pp. 103–10.

369a 'The world economic crisis and the empty circle' (An Islamic view), *Risalat al-Jihad* (Paola, Malta), No. 71, February 1989, pp. 146–53.

370 UPADHYA, K.K., 'Public economics of Islamic egalitarianism', *Journal of Objective Studies* (Aligarh), Vol. 1, No. 1–2, 1989, pp. 101–8.

371 USMANI, Muhammad Taqi, 'The role of religious boards in developing interest-free economy', *Al-Balagh* (Karachi), Vol. 1, No. 3, 1990, pp. 19–22.

372 No entry.

373 YUKAWA, Takeshi, 'State and society in medieval Islamic studies on the Iqta system in Arabic society' (Review article), *Annals of Japan Association for Middle East Studies*, No. 2, 1987, pp. 483–90.

374 ZAMAN, Hasanuz S.M., *The Economic Functions of the Early Islamic State*, Karachi: International Islamic Publications, 1981.

375 ZIADEH, Farhat J., Review article on *The Islamic Conception of Justice* by Majid Khadduri, in *Arab Studies Quarterly*, Vol. 8, No. 2, 1986, pp. 201–3.

Distributive Justice

376 ADAMS, Richard H. and ALDERMAN, Harold, 'Sources of income inequality in rural Pakistan: a decomposition analysis', *Oxford Bulletin of Economics and Statistics*, Vol. 54, No. 4, 1992, pp. 591–608.

377 AHMAD, Salahuddin, 'Principles of distribution in Islam', *Thoughts on Economics* (Dhaka), Vol. 8, No. 3–4, 1987, pp. 1–11.

378 AHMAD, Ziauddin, *Islam, Poverty and Income Distribution*, Leicester: Islamic Foundation, 1991.

379 CHOUDHURY, Masudul Alam, Review article on *Islam, Poverty and Income Distribution* by Ziauddin Ahmad, in *Hamdard Islamicus*, Vol. 15, No. 2, 1992, pp. 91–7.

380 HASAN, Zubair, 'Distributional equity in Islam', in Munawar Iqbal (ed.), *Distributive Justice and Need Fulfilment in an Islamic Economy*, Islamabad: International Institute of Islamic Economics, International Islamic University, 1986, pp. 25–54.

381 HOLLAND, Muhtar, *Public Duties in Islam: The Institution of the Hisba*, Leicester: Islamic Foundation, 1982.

382 IQBAL, Munawar (ed.), *Distributive Justice and Need Fulfilment in an Islamic Economy*, Islamabad: International Institute of Islamic Economics, International Islamic University, 1986, 278 pp.

383 MANNAN, M.A., 'Allocative efficiency, decision and welfare criteria in an interest-free Islamic economy: a comparative policy approach', in S. Tahir *et al.* (eds.), *Readings in Microeconomics: An Islamic Perspective*, Petaling Jaya: Longman Malaysia, 1992, pp. 220–38.

384 MANNAN, M.A., 'The economics of poverty in Islam with special reference to Muslim countries', in Munawar Iqbal (ed.), *Distributive Justice and Need Fulfilment in an Islamic Economy*, Islamabad: International Institute of Islamic Economics, International Islamic University, 1986, pp. 303–34.

385 RAZZAQUE, M.A., 'Distribution of wealth in Islam', in *Thoughts on Islamic Economics*, Dhaka: Islamic Economics Research Bureau, 1980, pp. 26–43.

386 SADEQ, A.H.M., 'Factor pricing and income distribution from an Islamic perspective', *Journal of Islamic Economics* (Kuala Lumpur), Vol. 2, No. 1, 1989, pp. 45–64.

387 SADEQ, A.H.M., 'Distribution of wealth through transfer payments', *Hamdard Islamicus* (Karachi), Vol. 12, No. 1, 1989, pp. 33–44.

388 SADEQ, Abdul Hasan M., 'Distribution of wealth in Islam', in *Thoughts on Islamic Economics*, Dhaka: Islamic Economics Research Bureau, 1980, pp. 45–63.

389 'Social justice through public administration: an Islamic perspective', *Al-Nahdah*, Vol. 10, No. 1–2, 1990, pp. 20–2.

390 ZARQA, Muhammad Anas, 'Islamic distributive schemes', in Munawar Iqbal (ed.), *Distributive Justice and Need Fulfilment in an Islamic Economy*, Islamabad: International Institute of Islamic Economics, International Islamic University, 1986, pp. 159–215.

Social and Economic Justice

391 AHMAD, Hasan, 'Social justice in Islam', *Islamic Studies* (Islamabad), No. 3, 1971, pp. 209–219.

392 AHMAD, Khurshid, *Social Justice in Islam*, Lahore: Institute of Islamic Culture, 1975.

393 AHMAD, Ziauddin, 'Socioeconomic values of Islam and their significance and relevance to the present day world', *Islamic Studies* (Islamabad), Vol. 10, No. 4, pp. 350–3.

394 AHMAD, Ziauddin, 'Islam and fulfilment of basic needs', *Islamic Order*, Vol. 9, No. 2, 1987, pp. 53–64.

395 AJMI, S.H., 'Traditional Islamic social welfare: its meaning, history and contemporary relevance', Part 1, *The Islamic Quarterly* (London), Vol. 35, No. 3, 1991, pp. 165–80.

396 AKRAI, Mohammad Saeed, 'The concept of Tawhid and social welfare in Islam', *Hamdard Islamicus* (Karachi), No. 4, 1988, pp. 73–6.

397 AMINUDDIN, M., 'The socio-economic order of Islam', *The Universal Message*, Vol. 9, No. 6, 1987, pp. 29–30.

398 BAKHASH, Shaul, 'Islam and social justice in Iran', in Martin Kramer (ed.), *Shiism, Resistance and Revolution*, London: Mansell, 1987, pp. 95–116.

399 BAKHASH, Shaul, 'The politics of land, law and social justice in Iran', *The Middle East Journal*, Vol. 43, No. 2, 1989, pp. 186–201.

400 BALOGUN, Ismail A.B., 'Some aspects of Islamic economics', in Ibrahim Sulaiman and Siraj Abdulkarim (eds.), *On the Political Future of Nigeria*, Zaria, Nigeria: Muslim Forum, 1988, pp. 48–55.

401 'Community development for the underprivileged and the poor', *Al-Nahdah Muslim News and Views*, Vol. 7, No. 4, 1987, pp. 7–11.

402 FAKHRY, Majid, Review of *The Islamic Conception of Justice, Al-Abhath* (Journal of the Centre for Arab and Middle East Studies), Vol. 34, 1986, pp. 63–9.

403 FAROOQUI, Muhammad, 'Belief, good conduct and economic welfare', *Islamic Order*, Vol. 8, No. 4, 1986, pp. 91–5.

404 GHIFARI, Nur Muhammad, *Social Security in Islam*, Lahore: Atiq Publication House, 1989.

405 GILANI, Shaukat J., 'The Qur'an on charitable giving and contemporary social values' (Notes), *Journal of Research in Islamic Economics*, Vol. 3, No. 1, 1985, pp. 63–74.

406 HASAN, A., 'Social justice in Islam', *Islamic Studies* (Islamabad), September 1971, pp. 209–19.

407 HASAN, Najmul, *Social Security System of Islam with Special Reference to Zakah*, Jeddah: International Centre for Research in Islamic Economics, 1984.

408 HUSAYN, Shaykh Shawkat, 'Non-Muslims and the law of social security in Islam', *Al-Tawhid* (Tehran), Vol. 6, No. 2, 1988–9, pp. 66–70.

409 KHADDURI, Majid, *The Islamic Conception of Justice*, Baltimore, MD: Johns Hopkins University Press, 1984, 256 pp.

410 KHAN, Muhammad, 'A comment on the notion of economic justice in contemporary Islamic thought', *International Journal of Middle East Studies*, Vol. 22, No. 3, 1990, pp. 375–6.

411 KINGBIERG, L., 'Compromise of commerce: a study of early traditions concerning poverty and wealth', *Der Islam* (Berlin), Vol. 66, No. 2, 1989, pp. 193–212.

412 KURAN, Timur, 'On the notion of economic justice in contemporary Islamic thought', *International Journal of Middle East Studies*, Vol. 21, 1989, pp. 171–91.

413 KURAN, Timur, 'Reply to Muhammad Khan's comment on the notion of economic justice in contemporary Islamic thought', *International Journal of Middle East Studies*, Vol. 22, No. 3, 1990, pp. 376–7.

414 MINTJES, H., *Social Justice in Islam*, Amsterdam: Institute for the Study of Religion, Free University, 1977.

415 MUSALLAM, Adnan A., 'Syed Qutb and social justice', *Journal of Islamic Studies*, Vol. 4, No. 1, 1993, pp. 52–70.

416 AL-NOWAIHI, Muhammad, 'Fundamentals of economic justice in Islam', in Muslim Students Association of the United States and Canada, *Contemporary Aspects of Economic Thinking in Islam*, Bloomington, IN: MSA, 1970, pp. 65–81.

417 NUR, Abdur, *Social Justice in Bangladesh: An Islamic Perspective*, Chittagong: University of Chittagong, 1991, 55 pp.

418 QURESHI, Anwar Iqbal, 'Islam's concept of life regarding economic matters', *Islamic Studies*, No. 11, December 1972, pp. 297–308.

419 RAHMAN, Tanzil-lur, 'Justice order', *Islamic Order* (Karachi), Vol. 11, No. 2, 1989, pp. 28–36.

420 SIDDIQI, M.N., 'Guarantee of a minimum level of living in an Islamic state', in Munawar Iqbal (ed.), *Distributive Justice and Need Fulfilment in an Islamic Economy*, Islamabad: International Institute of Islamic Economics, International Islamic University, 1986, pp. 249–84.

421 'The root cause of injustices of our time', *Al-Farooq* (Karachi), Vol. 4, No. 11, 1993, pp. 5–6.

422 YUSUF, S.M., *Economic Justice in Islam*, Lahore: Sh. Muhammad Ashraf, 1977.

7

LAND, LABOUR AND POPULATION

Land Tenure System

423 AHMAD, Qazi Masood, 'Comparative analysis of agricultural income tax with Ushr' (Pakistan), *Pakistan Economic and Social Review* (Lahore), Vol. 26, No. 2, 1988, pp. 109–66.

424 AMINI, Muhammad Taqi, *The Agrarian System of Islam*, Tr. Syed Ahmad Ali, New Delhi: Idarah-i Adabiyat-i Delhi, 1991, 275 pp.

425 GULAID, Mahmoud A., *Land Ownership in Islam: A Survey*, Jeddah: Islamic Development Bank, 1991, 46 pp.

426 GULAID, Mahmoud A., *Effect of Islamic Laws and Institutions on Land Tenure with Special Reference to Some Muslim Countries*, Jeddah: Islamic Development Bank, 1990, 59 pp.

427 HAJRAH, Hassan Hamza, *Public Land Distribution in Saudi Arabia*, London: Longman, 1992.

428 HAQUE, Ziaul, *Landlord and Peasant in Early Islam*, Islamabad: Islamic Research Institute.

429 HOQUE, Monjurul, 'Land administration in Islam – a second view of As-Sawad', *Thoughts on Economics* (Dhaka), Vol. 1, 1991, pp. 65–80.

430 HUSSAIN, Zakir, 'The working of Jagir system in the Deccan during last years of Aurangzeb' (Feudal system, Mughal India), *Journal of Objective Studies* (Aligarh), Vol. 2, No. 2, 1990, pp. 72–80.

431 JOHANSEN, Baber, *The Islamic Law on Land Tax and Rent: The Peasants' Loss of Property Rights Under the Hanafite Doctrine in the Mameluke and Ottoman Periods*, Exeter Arabic and Islamic Series, London: Croom Helm, 1988.

432 KENNEDY, Charles H., 'Islamization of real estate: pre-emption and land reforms in Pakistan, 1978–1992', *Journal of Islamic Studies*, Vol. 4, No. 1, 1993, pp. 71–83.

433 KHALIDI, Tariq (ed.), *Land Tenure and Social Transformation in the Middle East*, Beirut: American University of Beirut, 1984.

434 KHAN, Shahrukh Rafi, 'Henry George and an alternative Islamic land tenure system', *Economic Development and Cultural Change*, Vol. 36, No. 4, 1988, pp. 721–89.

435 MOOSVI, S., 'Magnitude of land revenues, demand and income of the Mughal ruling class under Akbar', in *Medieval India: A Miscellany*, No. 4, Aligarh, 1977.

436 REILLY, James A., 'Shari'ah court registers and land tenure around nineteenth-century Damascus', *Middle East Studies Association Bulletin*, Vol. 21, No. 2, 1987, pp. 155–69.

437 SCHIRAZI, A., *The Problem of Land Reform in the Islamic Republic of Iran: Complications and Consequences of an Islamic Policy*, Occasional Paper No. 10 of the Freie Universität Berlin, Berlin: Das Arabische Buch, 1987, 71 pp.

438 SCHOLCH, Alexander, 'Was there a feudal system in Ottoman Lebanon and Palestine?', in David Kushner (ed.), *Palestine in the Late Ottoman Period*, Leiden: Brill, 1986, pp. 130–45.

439 UBAYDLI, Ahmad, 'The agrarian economy of Oman (132–280/749–893) in Arabic sources', *Journal of Islamic Studies*, Vol. 4, No. 1, 1993, pp. 33–51.

440 WILKINSON, John C., 'Muslim land and water law', *Journal of Islamic Studies* (Oxford), Vol. 1, 1990, pp. 54–72.

Labour and Wages

441 AHMAD, Ziauddin, 'Employer–worker relationship in Islam', *Islamic Order*, Vol. 8, No. 4, 1986, pp. 22–41.

442 ALI, Ali Abdalla, 'How to reach the small farmer? – an Islamic formula', *IFDA Dossier* (International Foundation for Development Alternatives, Nyon, Switzerland), No. 75–6, January–April 1990, pp. 35–44.

443 'Dignity of labour in Islam', *The Concept* (London), No. 11, November 1991, pp. 19–20.

444 EGAMI, Tomoyuki, *Labour and Action in Islam: Searching for an Outlook on Last Labour*, Working Paper Series No. 21, Tokyo: Institute of Middle Eastern Studies, 1990.

445 FARIDI, F.R., 'On wages in an Islamic economy', *Islamic Thought* (Aligarh), April 1960, pp. 61–6.

446 IQBAL, Afzal, 'Response of Islam to industrial and post-industrial challenge', *Islamic Studies*, Vol. 25, No. 1, 1986, pp. 76–91.

447 KHAN, Farouk, 'Wealth, labour and savings' (An Islamic view), *The American Journal of Islamic Finance* (Rancho Palos Verdes, CA), Vol. 2, No. 3, 1992, pp. 9–11.

448 EL-QUDAH, Zakariya, 'Work and its perfection from a Muslim point of view' (Including comment), in *Common Humanitarian Ideals for Muslims and Christians*, Proceedings of the Fourth Muslim–Christian Consultation, Amman, Jordan, Vol. 2, Amman: Royal Academy for Islamic Civilization Research (Al-Albait Foundation), 1987, pp. 7–38.

449 SULTAN, Lotfi Ali, 'The dignity of labour (Islamic viewpoint)', *Al-Azhar Magazine* (Cairo), Vol. 64, No. 7, 1992, pp. 855–58.

450 WENDEN, Catherine Withol de, 'Trade unions, Islam and immigration', *Economic and Industrial Democracy: An International Journal*, Vol. 9, February 1988, pp. 65–82.

451 ZUBAIR, A., 'Concept and protection of labour under Islamic law', *Islamic Order* (Karachi), No. 3, 1989, pp. 18–24.

Population and Employment

452 AGHAJANIAN, Akbar, 'Population policy, fertility and family planning in Iran', in K. Mahadevan (ed.), *Fertility Policies of Asian Countries*, London: Sage, 1989, pp. 228–47.

453 AKHTAR, M. Ramzan, 'An Islamic framework for employer–employee relationship', *The American Journal of Islamic Social Sciences* (Herndon, VA), Vol. 9, No. 2, 1992, pp. 202–18.

454 ANEES, Munawar Ahmad, 'Birth control: the Islamic juridical view', *Islamic and Comparative Law Quarterly* (New Delhi), No. 83, 1988, pp. 233–43.

455 AZID, Toseef, 'Unemployment and its solution in Islam', *Journal of Rural Development and Administration* (Peshawar), Vol. 21, No. 1, 1989, pp. 65–77.

456 BAH, Sulaiman M., 'Mortality and morbidity in Muslim populations: a framework for the reduction of their factors', *Hamdard Islamicus* (Karachi), Vol. 15, No. 2, 1992, pp. 75–86.

457 BALOGUN, Ismail A.B., 'Muslim attitude to family planning', *Journal of Arabic and Religious Studies*, Vol. 3, 1986, pp. 24–35.

458 BUDHRAM, Dowlat Ram, 'Muslim participation in the manufacturing sector of Guyana', *Journal Institute of Muslim Minority Affairs*, Vol. 4, No. 1–2, 1982, pp. 194–202.

459 FARUK, Alhaji Usman, *Family Planning: The Islamic View Point*, Kaduna, Nigeria: Paragon Publisher and Printer, 1989, 32 pp.
460 OMRAN, Abdel Rahim, *Family Planning in the Legacy of Islam*, London: Routledge, 1992, 284 pp.
461 SAID, Hakim Muhammad, *The Employer and the Employee: Islamic Concept*, Karachi: Hamdard Academy, 1972.

8

ISLAMIC CRITIQUE OF OTHER ECONOMIC SYSTEMS

General

462 ABDUL-RAUF, Muhammad, 'Islam and contemporary economic system', in *Contemporary Aspects of Economic Thinking in Islam*, Proceedings of the Third East Coast Regional Conference of the Muslim Students Association of the United States and Canada, April 1968, Plainsfield, IN: American Trust Publications, 1970, 1980, pp. 51–6.

463 ABDUL-WAHID, Ahmad, 'Islam and contemporary economic theories', *The Muslim World League Journal* (Makkah), Rabial-Thari 1405, p. 36.

464 ABU-SAUD, Mahmoud, *Economics within Transcendence* (An Islamic approach), Herndon, VA: International Institute of Islamic Thought, 1990.

465 AHMAD, Shaikh Mahmud, *Economics of Islam: A Comparative Study*, Lahore: Ashraf, 1977.

466 ALI, Ausaf, Review article on *Islam and the Economic Challenge* by M. Umer Chapra, in *Hamdard Islamicus*, Vol. 16, No. 4, 1993, pp. 127–48.

467 AL-ARABI, M.A., *The Islamic Economy and Contemporary Economy*, Proceedings of the First Conference of the Academy of Islamic Research, Cairo: Al-Azhar, 1964.

468 EL-BANNA, Gamel, 'The crisis of unionism between contemporary ideologies and Islam', *Islamic Quarterly*, Vol. 30, No. 1, 1986, pp. 5–19.

469 ISMAIL, Syed Muhammad, *Critical Analysis of Capitalism, Socialism and Islamic Economic Order*, Lahore: Oriental Publications, 1989, 570 pp.

470 KHAN, Mehr Muhammad Nawaz, *Islam and Other Economic Systems*, Lahore: Islamic Book Service, 1988.

471 MASTERS, Bruce, *The Origins of Western Economic Dominance in the Middle East: Mercantilism and the Islamic Economy*, New York: New York University Press, 1988, 240 pp.
472 MUZAMMIL, Mohammad, 'Smithian concept of economic behaviour and Islam', *Journal of Objective Studies* (Aligarh), Vol. 3, No. 2, 1991, pp. 39–47.
473 RAUF, M.A., *The Islamic Economic Doctrine and Contemporary Thought*, Washington, DC: American Enterprise Institute for Public Policy Research.
474 AL-SADR, Muhammad Baqir, *Islam and Schools of Economics*, Albany, NY: Persian Speaking Group, Muslim Students Association, 1984.
475 SHARIF, M. Raihan, 'Compatibility of the socio-economic system – as a base for enduring ideology', *Thoughts on Economics* (Dhaka), Vol. 1, No. 1, 1991, pp. 1–30.
476 SIDDIQI, Muhammad Nejatullah, 'An Islamic approach to economics', *Al-Tawhid*, Vol. 4, No. 2, 1986–7, pp. 105–25.
477 The Muslim Students Association of the United States and Canada, *Contemporary Aspects of Economic Thinking in Islam*, Bloomington, IN: MSA, 1976.
478 VADILLO, Umar, *The End of Economics: An Islamic Critique of Economics*, San Gregorio, Granada: Madinah Press, 1991.

Capitalism

479 ABBASI, M.A., 'Interest – an economic study on the three economic systems: capitalism, socialism and Islam', *The Islamic Review of Arab Affairs*, Vol. 57, March–April 1968, pp. 28–32.
480 ABDUL-RAUF, Muhammad, *The Islamic Doctrine of Economics and Contemporary Economic Thought: Highlights of a Conference on Theological Inquiry into Capitalism and Socialism*, Washington, DC: American Enterprise Institute, 1979.
481 ABDUL-RAUF, Muhammad, *A Muslim's Reflections on Democratic Capitalism*, Washington, DC: American Enterprise Institute for Public Policy Research, 1984.
482 BEININ, Joel, 'Islamic responses to the capitalist penetration of the Middle East', in Barbara Freyer Stowasser (ed.), *The Islamic Impulse*, London: Croom Helm, 1987, pp. 87–105.
483 BELOKRENITSKI, Viacheslav Y., *Capitalism in Pakistan*, New Delhi: Patriot Publishers, 1991, 370 pp.

484 BERGER, Peter L. (ed.), *The Capitalist Spirit: Toward a Religious Ethic of Wealth Creation*, San Francisco: ICS Press, 1990, 192 pp.

485 CLAMMER, John, *Islam and Capitalism in South East Asia*, Working Paper No. 63, Singapore: Department of Sociology, Singapore University, 1978.

486 JOMO, K.S., 'Islam and Weber: Rodinson on the implication of religion for capitalist development', *Developing Economies*, Vol. 15, No. 2, 1977, pp. 240–50.

487 JOMO, K.S., 'Islam and capitalist development: a critique of Rodinson and Weber', in K.S. Jomo (ed.), *Islamic Economic Alternatives*, London: Macmillan, 1992, pp. 125–38.

488 KURAN, Timur, Review article on *Islam and the Economic Challenge* by M. Umer Chapra, in *Journal of Economic Literature*, Vol. 31, No. 3, 1993, pp. 1484–6.

489 LABIB, Subhi Y., 'Capitalism in medieval Islam', *Journal of Economic History*, Vol. 29, 1969, pp. 77–98.

490 RENFO, Raymond and ZAFAR, Hannan, 'Capitalistic elements in Islamic thought', *Economic Forum*, Vol. 11, No. 1, pp. 79–88.

491 RODINSON, Maxime, *Islam and Capitalism*, tr. Brian Pearce, London: Allen Lane, 1974.

492 TURNER, Bryan S., *Weber and Islam: A Critical Study*, London: Routledge and Kegan Paul, 1974.

493 TURNER, Bryan S., 'Islam, capitalism and Weber thesis', *British Journal of Sociology*, Vol. 25, No. 2, 1974, pp. 230–43.

494 WALKOM, Tom, 'Fundamentalism: market mullahs' (A critique of capitalism), *New Internationalist*, No. 210, August 1990, pp. 12–13.

Socialism

495 GELLNER, Ernest, 'Islam and Marxism: some comparisons', *International Affairs* (Cambridge), Vol. 67, No. 1, 1990, pp. 1–6.

496 HUSSAIN, M.M., *Islam and Socialism: A Critical Study of Socialism, Capitalism and Fascism as Contrasted with the Qur'anic Concept of a New World Order*, Lahore: Ashraf, 1970.

497 MUHAMMAD, Ismail, *Critical Analysis of Capitalism, Socialism and Islamic Economic Order*, Lahore: Oriental Publications, 1989, 570 pp.

498 MURADPURI, Muhammad Akbar, *Conflict between Socialism and Islam*, Lahore: Ashraf, 1970.

Islamic Theory of Ownership

499 ABE, T., *A Comparative Study of Islamic Ownership: Conceptual Frameworks of Ownership in Islamic and Western Value Systems*, Niigata, Japan: Institute of Middle Eastern Studies, 1987.

500 AMIN, S.H., 'Intellectual property rights in Islam: the experience of Saudi Arabia and the United Arab Emirates', *Muslim Education Quarterly* (Cambridge), Vol. 7, No. 1, 1989, pp. 42–58.

501 AWAN, Akhtar A., *Equality, Efficiency and Property Ownership in the Islamic System*, New York: Lanham, for University Press of America, 1983.

502 AZAD, Ghulam Murtaza and ZAMAN, S.M., 'The question of *Milk*' (Ownership in Waqf), *The Muslim World League Journal* (Makkah), Vol. 11–12, 1988, pp. 17–20.

503 AZMIN, Z.H.U., 'Ownership of land in Islam', *The Law Majallah* (Law Society, International Islamic University, Malaysia), 1987, pp. 65–80.

504 BEHDAD, Sohrab, 'Property rights and Islamic economic approaches', in K.S. Jomo (ed.), *Islamic Economic Alternatives*, London: Macmillan, 1992, pp. 77–104.

505 BUANG, Sallch, 'The law of real property in Malaysia: prospects for Islamization', *IIU Law Journal* (Petaling Jaya), Vol. 1, No. 1, 1989, pp. 83–112.

506 FAROOQ, M. Omar, 'Public vs private sector: policy dynamics in an Islamic perspective', *Thoughts on Economics* (Dhaka), Vol. 1, No. 2–3, 1991, pp. 27–32.

507 GACEK, A., 'Ownership statements and seals in Arabic manuscripts', *Manuscripts of the Middle East* (Leiden), No. 2, 1987, pp. 88–95.

508 HOSSEINI, Hamid, 'Notions of private property in Islamic economics', *International Journal of Social Economics*, Spring 1989.

509 HOWARD-MERRIUM, K., 'Egyptian Islamism and the law: connecting the "private" and the "public"', *International Journal of Islamic and Arabic Studies* (Bloomington, IN), Vol. 5, No. 1, 1988, pp. 77–96.

510 ISHAQUE, K.M., 'Private property and its role in Islamic social order', in *Economic System of Islam*, Karachi: National Bank of Pakistan, 1980, pp. 19–54.

511 KHAN, Mohammad, Review article on *Islam, Poverty and Income Distribution* by Ziauddin Ahmad, in *Review of Islamic Economics*, Vol. 2, No. 1, 1992, pp. 55–7.

512 MIRAKHOR, Abbas, 'Property ownership: a right guaranteed by Islam for individual's creative labour', *Crescent*, Vol. 16, No. 24, March 1988, pp. 7, 11.

513 MUSTAFA, Ahmad H. and ASKARI, Hossein G., 'Economic implications of land ownership and land cultivation in Islam', in Munawar Iqbal (ed.), *Distributive Justice and Need Fulfilment in an Islamic Economy*, Islamabad: International Institute of Islamic Economics, 1986, pp. 85–141.

514 SADEQ, A.H.M., 'Distribution of wealth through transfer payments', *Hamdard Islamicus* (Karachi), Vol. 12, No. 1, 1989, pp. 33–44.

515 SAKR, Mohammad Ahmad, 'Islamic concept of ownership and its economic implications', in A. Ahmad and K.R. Awan (eds.), *Lectures on Islamic Economics*, Jeddah: Islamic Development Bank, 1992, pp. 117–30.

516 SHAFI, Mufti Muhammad, *Distribution of Wealth in Islam*, Karachi: Begum Aisha Bawany Wakf, 1975.

517 SHAFI, Mufti Muhammad, 'Distribution of wealth in Islam', Part 1, tr. M.H. Askari, *Al-Balagh International* (Karachi), Vol. 2, No. 4, 1991, pp. 8–19.

518 TALEQANI, Sayyed Mahmud, *Islam and Ownership*, tr. Ahmad Jabbari and Farhang Rajaee, Lexington, KY: Mazda Publishers, 1983.

9

ECONOMIC HISTORY OF THE MUSLIM PEOPLE

Early Muslim Economic History

519 EL-ALI, S.A., 'Muslim estates in Hidjaz in the first century AH', *Journal of the Economic and Social History of the Orient* (Leiden), Vol. 2, Part 1, 1959, pp. 247–61.

520 BAGCHI, A.K., 'The Mughal economy: a quantitative study' (Review article), *The Indian Historical Review* (New Delhi), Vol. 13, No. 2, 1986–7, pp. 174–80.

521 BARABOUND, Mohammad, 'Economic trends in Al-Andulus during the period of the Taifah states', *Islamic Studies*, Vol. 30, No. 1–4, 1991, pp. 213–40.

522 BONNE, Alfred, *States and Economics in the Middle East*, Westport, CT: Greenwood Press, 1973.

523 COHEN, Amnon, *Economic Life in Ottoman Jerusalem*, Cambridge Studies in Islamic Civilization, Cambridge: Cambridge University Press, 1989, 187 pp.

524 COHEN, J. Hayyim, 'The economic background and the secular occupation of Muslim jurisprudents and traditionalists in the classical period of Islam' (Until the middle of the eleventh century), *Journal of the Economic and Social History of the Orient* (Leiden), Vol. 12, Part 1, 1970, p. 161.

525 DJANDJGAVA, G., 'Ways of estimation of the population numbers of the medieval Islamic cities based on the example of Fustat Cairo', in *BRISMES Proceedings of the 1991 International Conference on Middle Eastern Studies*, Oxford: British Society for Middle East Studies, 1991, pp. 231–7.

526 FINDLEY, Carter Vaughan, 'Economic basis of revolution and repression in the late Ottoman empire', *Comparative Studies in Society and History*, Vol. 28, No. 1, 1986, pp. 81–106.

527 GOITEIN, S.D., *A Mediterranean Society*, Vol. 1, *Economic Foundation – The Jewish Communities of the Arab World as Portrayed in the Documents of the Cairo Geniza*, Berkeley, CA: University of California Press, 1967.

528 GRICE-HUTCHINSON, Marjorie, *Early Economic Thought in Spain, 1177–1740*, London: Allen and Unwin, 1978.

529 HABIB, Irfan, 'Potentialities of capitalistic development in the economy of Mughal India', *Journal of Economic History*, Vol. 29, No. 1, 1969.

530 HABIB, Irfan, *Peasants and Artisan Resistance in Mughal India*, McGill Studies in International Development No. 34, Montreal: Center for Developing Area Studies, McGill University, 1984.

531 IBRAHIM, Mahmood, 'Social and economic conditions in pre-Islamic Mecca', *International Journal of Middle East Studies*, Vol. 14, 1982, pp. 343–58.

532 INLACIK, Halil, 'Jews in the Ottoman economy and finances, 1450–1500', in C.E. Bosworth *et al* (eds.), *The Islamic World: From Classical to Modern Times (Essays in Honor of Bernard Lewis)*, Princeton, NJ: Darwin Press, 1989, pp. 171–7.

533 ISLAM, Riazul, 'Aspects of 'Ala Ud-Din Khalji's economic policy and its impact' (With special reference to the fixation of prices) (14th-century India), *Journal of Central Asia* (Islamabad), Vol. 12, No. 2, 1989, pp. 5–20.

534 ISLAM, Riazul, 'Some aspects of the economy of Northern South Asia during the fourteenth century', *Journal of Central Asia* (Islamabad), Vol. 11, No. 2, 1988, pp. 5–28.

535 ISLAM, Zafrul, 'The Mughal system of escheat and the Islamic law of inheritance', *Islamic Culture* (Hyderabad), Vol. 62, No. 4, 1988, pp. 23–36.

536 JENNINGS, Ronald C., 'Pious foundations in the society and economy of Ottoman Tarbazon, 1565–1640', *Journal of the Economic and Social History of the Orient* (Leiden), Vol. 33, No. 3, 1990, pp. 271–336.

537 LECKKER, Michael, 'The estates of 'Amr b. al-As in Palestine: notes on a new Negev inscription', *Bulletin of the School of Oriental and African Studies* (London), Vol. 52, No. 1, 1989, pp. 24–37.

538 MARTINAZ, A.P., 'Atavistic and negotiation states, and command and market economies in Middle Eastern history with particular reference to Ottoman Empire', *Archivum Ottomanicum* (Wiesbaden), Vol. 12, 1987, pp. 105–75.

539 MASTERS, Bruce, *The Origins of Western Economic Dominance in the Middle East: Mercantilism and the Islamic Economy in Aleppo, 1600–1750*, New York: New York University Press, 1987, 320 pp.

540 MOGHADAM, Fatemehe, 'Property rights and Islamic revolution in Iran', in Haleh Esfandiari and A.L. Udovitch (eds.), *The Economic Dimensions of Middle Eastern History*, Princeton, NJ: Darwin Press, 1990, pp. 147–78.

541 MOOSVI, Shireen, 'The gross national product of the Mughal empire, *c.* 1660', *The Indian Historical Review* (New Delhi), Vol. 13, No. 1–2, 1986–7, pp. 75–87.

542 NAQVI, Hamida Khatoon, *Agricultural, Industrial and Urban Dynamism under the Sultans of Delhi, 1206–1555*, New Delhi: Munshiram Manoharlal Publishers, 1986, 205 pp.

543 O'BRIEN, George, *An Essay on Medieval Economic Teaching*, London: Longmans Green, 1920.

544 OGUZ, Orhand and TABAKOGLU, Ahmad, 'An historical approach to Islamic pricing policy: research on the Ottoman price system and its application', *Journal of King Abdul Aziz University: Islamic Economics* (Jeddah), Vol. 3, 1991, pp. 65–80.

545 OKYAR, Osman, 'Economic growth in the Ottoman empire, 1800–1914', *Asian and African Studies*, Vol. 21, No. 1, 1987, pp. 87–118.

546 QAISAR, A.J., 'The role of brokers in medieval India', *Indian Historical Review* (New Delhi), Vol. 1, No. 2, 1974.

547 QUATAERT, D., 'The employment policies of the Ottoman public debt administration, 1881–1909', *Wiener Zeitschrift für die Kunde des Morgenlandes*, No. 76, 1986, pp. 233–7.

548 RANA, Irfan Mahmud, *Economic System under Omar the Great*, Lahore: Ashraf, 1970, 152 pp.

549 RODINSON, Maxime, *Islam and Capitalism*, tr. Brian Pearce, London: Allen Lane, 1974.

550 ROGAN, E.L., 'Money-lending and capital flows from Nublus, Damascus and Jerusalem to Qada al-Salt in the last decades of Ottoman rule', in T. Philipp (ed.), *The Syrian Land in the Eighteenth Century*, Stuttgart: Steiner, 1992, pp. 239–60.

551 TUMA, Elias, 'Early Arab economic policies, 1st–7th and 4th–10th centuries', *Islamic Studies*, Vol. 6, No. 1, 1965, pp. 1–23.

552 ZAMAN, Hasanuz S.M., *The Economic Functions of the Early Islamic State*, Karachi: International Islamic Publishers, 1981.

Muslim Economic Thought

553 ABD'ALLAH, Umar, 'Malik's concept of Amal', Ph.D. dissertation, University of Chicago, 1978.

554 ALATAS, Syed Faris, 'Ibn Khaldun and the modes of production in Ottoman Turkey and Safavid Iran', *Alserat* (London), Vol. 15, 1989, pp. 3–38.

555 BALJON, J.M.S., 'Social and economic ideas of Shah Wali Allah' (18th-century revivalist), in A.H.M. Sadeq and A. Ghazali (eds.), *Readings in Islamic Economic Thought*, Petaling Jaya: Longman Malaysia, 1992, pp. 238–45.

556 BOULAKIA, Jean David C., 'Ibn Khaldun: a fourteenth-century economist', *Journal of Political Economy*, Vol. 75, No. 5, 1971, pp. 1105–18.

557 GHAZALI, Aidit, 'Economic thought of Ibn Hazm' (10th-century scholar), in A.H.M. Sadeq and A. Ghazali (eds.), *Readings in Islamic Economic Thought*, Petaling Jaya: Longman Malaysia, 1992, pp. 66–73.

558 GHAZALI, Aidit, 'Economic significance in Ibn Tufayl's philosophy' (13th-century philosopher), in A.H.M. Sadeq and A. Ghazali (eds.), *Readings in Islamic Economic Thought*, Petaling Jaya: Longman Malaysia, 1992, pp. 111–18.

559 GHAZALI, Aidit, 'Economic thought of Abd Allah Harith al-Muhasibi' (9th-century jurist), in A.H.M. Sadeq and A. Ghazali (eds.), *Readings in Islamic Economic Thought*, Petaling Jaya: Longman Malaysia, 1992, pp. 59–65.

560 GHAZALI, Aidit, 'Economic thought of Nizam Al Tjusi' (11th-century statesman), in A.H.M. Sadeq and A. Ghazali (eds.), *Readings in Islamic Economic Thought*, Petaling Jaya: Longman Malaysia, 1992, pp. 74–87.

561 GHAZANFAR, S.M. and ISLAHI, A. Azim, 'Economic thought of an Arab scholastic: Abu Hamid Al-Ghazali', *History of Political Economy* (Durham, NC), 1990, pp. 381–403.

562 ISLAHI, Abdul Azim, 'Ibn Taimiyyah's concept of market mechanism', *Journal of Research in Islamic Economics*, Winter 1985, pp. 55–64.

563 ISLAHI, Abdul Azim, *Economic Concepts of Ibn Taimiyyah*, Leicester: Islamic Foundation, 1988.

564 ISLAHI, Abdul Azim, 'Shah Wali Allah's concept of Al Irtifaqat: stages of socio-economic development', *Journal of Objective Studies* (Aligarh), Vol. 2, No. 1, 1990, pp. 46–63.

565 No entry.

566 ISLAHI, Abdul Azim, 'Economic concepts of Ibn Taimiyyah' (13th-century revivalist), in A.H.M. Sadeq and A. Ghazali (eds.), *Readings in Islamic Economic Thought*, Petaling Jaya: Longman Malaysia, 1992, pp. 119–56.

567 ISLAHI, Abdul Azim, 'Economic concepts of Ibn Al Qayyim' (14th-century scholar), in A.H.M. Sadeq and A. Ghazali (eds.), *Readings in Islamic Economic Thought*, Petaling Jaya: Longman Malaysia, 1992, pp. 157–75.

568 ISLAHI, Abdul Azim, 'Ibn Taimiyyah's concept of market mechanism', in S. Tahir *et al.* (eds.), *Readings in Microeconomics: An Islamic Perspective*, Petaling Jaya: Longman Malaysia, 1992, pp. 157–64.

569 ISSAWI, Charles, 'Ibn Khaldun's analysis of economic issues' (14th-century historian), in A.H.M. Sadeq and A. Ghazali (eds.), *Readings in Islamic Economic Thought*, Petaling Jaya: Longman Malaysia, 1992, pp. 222–37.

570 JALBANI, G.N., 'The socio-economic thought of Shah Wali Allah', in A.H.M. Sadeq and A. Ghazali (eds.), *Readings in Islamic Economic Thought*, Petaling Jaya: Longman Malaysia, 1992, pp. 246–59.

571 MANZAR, A.M., 'Islamic economic system as reflected in the writings of Maulana Maududi', *Radiance Views Weekly* (Delhi), Vol. 25, No. 6, 1989, pp. 6–8.

572 MEYER, M.S., 'Economic thought in the Ottoman empire from the 14th to early 19th centuries', *Archiv Orientalni* (Prague), Vol. 4, No. 57, 1989, pp. 305–318.

573 MIRAKHOR, Abbas, 'The Muslim scholar and the history of economics: a need for consideration', *The American Journal of Islamic Social Sciences*, Vol. 4, No. 2, 1987, pp. 245–76.

574 SADEQ, Abul Hasan M., 'Al Ghazali on economic issues and some ethico-juristic matters having implications for economic behaviour', in A.H.M. Sadeq and A. Ghazali (eds.), *Readings in Islamic Economic Thought*, Petaling Jaya: Longman Malaysia, 1992, pp. 88–110.

575 SADEQ, Abul Hasan M., 'Islamic economic thought' (Introduction), in A.H.M. Sadeq and A. Ghazali (eds.), *Readings in Islamic Economic Thought*, Petaling Jaya: Longman Malaysia, 1992, pp. 1–13.

576 SADEQ, Abul Hasan M. and GHAZALI, Aidit (eds.), *Readings in Islamic Economic Thought*, Petaling Jaya: Longman Malaysia, 1992, 272 pp.

577 SATTAR, M. Abdus, 'Ibn Khaldun's contribution to economic thought', in Muslim Students Association of the United States and Canada, *Contemporary Aspects of Economic Thinking in Islam*, Indianapolis: American Trust Publications, 1980.

578 SIDDIQI, Muhammad Nejatullah, 'Islamic economic thought: foundations, evolution and needed direction', in A.H.M. Sadeq and A. Ghazali (eds.), *Readings in Islamic Economic Thought*, Petaling Jaya: Longman Malaysia, 1992, pp. 14–32.

579 SIDDIQI, Muhammad Nejatullah, 'History of Islamic economic thought', *Aligarh Journal of Islamic Thought* (Aligarh), No. 1, 1988, pp. 24–43.

580 SPENGLER, Joseph, 'Economic thought of Islam: Ibn Khaldun', *Comparative Studies in Society and History*, Vol. 6, No. 3, p. 270.

Early Islamic Trade and Commerce

581 CRONE, Patricia, *Meccan Trade and the Rise of Islam*, Princeton, NJ: Princeton University Press, 1986.

582 CRONE, Patricia, 'Serjeant and Meccan trade' (A bibliography), *Arabica* (Leiden), Vol. 39, No. 2, 1992, pp. 216–40.

583 FLOOR, Willem, 'A report on the trade in Jedda in the 1730s', *Money: Orient and Ocean* (Paris), Vol. 5, 1988, pp. 161–73.

584 GOFFMAN, Daniel, 'Izmir and the Levantine world, 1550–1650' (17th-century trade centre in Ottoman Turkey), Seattle, WA: University of Washington, 1990, 280 pp.

585 GUSAU, Sule Ahmad, 'Economic views of Ibn Khaldun', *Journal of Objective Studies* (Aligarh), Vol. 3, No. 2, 1991, pp. 48–66.

586 HASAN, Abdullah Alwi Haj, 'The Arabian commercial background in pre-Islamic times', *Islamic Culture* (Hyderabad), Vol. 61, No. 2, 1987, pp. 70–83.

587 HASHMI, S. Wajid, 'Trading: an Islamic outlook', *The Universal Message*, Vol. 8, No. 10, 1987, pp. 31–3.

588 HATHAWAY, Jane, 'A twelfth-century partnership in silk-trading in the Egyptian delta: a Geniza study', *The Journal of the Middle Eastern Studies Society at Columbia University* (New York), Vol. 2, No. 1, 1988, pp. 23–7.

589 HUSSEIN, Raef T.A., 'The early Arabian trade and marketing', *Islamic Culture* (Hyderabad), Vol. 59, No. 4, 1985, pp. 365–76.

590 HUSSEIN, Raef T.A., 'The early Arabian trade and marketing', *Islamic Quarterly*, Vol. 30, No. 2, 1986, pp. 109–17.

591 HUSSEIN, Raef T.A., 'The early Arabian trade and marketing', *Islam and the Modern Age*, May–August 1987, pp. 163–72.

592 IRVAN, N., 'Illegal local trade in the Ottoman empire and the guilds of Istanbul, 1725–26: suggested new hypothesis', *International Journal of Turkish Studies* (Madison, WI), Vol. 5, No. 1–2, 1992, pp. 1–26.

593 KISTER, M.J., 'The market of the Prophet', *Journal of the Economic and Social History of the Orient* (Leiden), Vol. 8, No.3, 1965, pp. 272–6.

594 LECKER, M. 'On the market of Medina (Yathrib) in pre-Islamic and early Islamic times', *Jerusalem Studies in Arabic and Islam*, No. 8, Part 1, 1986, pp. 133–47.

595 LIEBER, Alfred E., 'Eastern business practices and medieval European commerce', *Journal of Economic History Review*, 1968, pp. 230–43.

596 LOWICK, Nicholas, *Islamic Coins and Trade in the Medieval World*, Aldershot: Variorum, 1990, 304 pp.

597 MITCHINER, Michael, 'Evidence for Viking–Islamic trade provided by Samavid silver coinage', *East and West* (Rome), Vol. 37, No. 1–4, 1987, pp. 39–50.

598 MORTEL, Richard T., 'Prices in Mecca during the Mamluk period', *Journal of the Economic and Social History of the Orient* (Leiden), Vol. 32, No. 3, 1989, pp. 279–334.

599 MOURIAUX, René and WENDEN, Catherine Withol de, *French Trade Unionism and Islam*, Muslims in Europe Research Papers, No. 36, 1987, 35 pp.

600 MUGHAL, Mohammad Rafique, 'Early Muslim cities in Sindh and pattern of international trade', *Islamic Studies*, Vol. 31, No. 3, 1992, pp. 267–86.

601 MUNEM, Shaker Mahmoud Abdul, 'Trade routes during the Abbasid Era and the importance of the capital Baghdad', *Journal of Central Asia* (Islamabad), Vol. 13, No. 1, 1990, pp. 218–26.

602 PETERS, F.E., 'The commerce of Mecca before Islam', in Farhad Kazemi and R.D. McChesney (eds.), *A Way Prepared: Essays on Islamic Culture in Honor of Richard Bayley Winder*, New York: New York University Press, 1988, pp. 3–26.

603 RICHARDS, D.S. (ed.), *Islam and the Trade of Asia*, Oxford: Bruno Cassirer Press, 1970.

604 RISSO, Patricia, 'Muslim identity in maritime trade: general observation and some evidence from the eighteenth-century Persian Gulf/Indian Ocean region', *International Journal of Middle East Studies*, Vol. 21, No. 3, 1989, pp. 381–92.

605 RUBIN, Uri, 'Meccan trade and Quranic exegesis', *Bulletin of the School of Oriental and African Studies* (London), Vol. 53, No. 3, 1990, pp. 421–8.
606 SPULER, Bertold, 'Trade in the eastern Islamic countries in the early centuries', in D.S. Richards (ed.), *Islam and the Trade of Asia*, Oxford: Bruno Cassirer Press, 1970, pp. 11–20.
607 UDOVITCH, A.L., 'Commercial techniques in early medieval Islamic trade', in D.S. Richards (ed.), *Islam and the Trade of Asia*, Oxford: Bruno Cassirer Press, 1970, pp. 37–62.
608 UDOVITCH, A.L., 'Commerce and society in mid-eleventh-century Egypt and North Africa', in Haleh Esfandiari and A.L. Udovitch (eds.), *The Economic Dimensions of Middle Eastern History*, Princeton, NJ: Darwin Press, 1990, pp. 239–54.
609 ZAMAN, Muhammad Q., 'Merchant capital and Islam' (Review article), *The American Journal of Islamic Social Sciences* (Herndon, VA), Vol. 8, No. 3, 1991, pp. 557–61.
610 No entry.

Part II

MONEY, BANKING AND FINANCE

10

ISLAMIC CONCEPT OF MONEY, INTEREST AND PROFIT

Concept of Money

611 ABU SAUD, Mahmoud, 'Money, interest and Qirad', in Khurshid Ahmad (ed.), *Studies in Islamic Economics*, Jeddah: International Centre for Research in Islamic Economics, King Abdul Aziz University, 1980, pp. 59–83.

612 AHMAD, Sheikh Mahmood, 'Man and money', *Islamic Studies*, Vol. 9, September 1970, pp. 217–44.

613 HUSSAIN, S. Mushtaq, 'Interest on money and Islam: a suggested analysis', in *Report of First Regional Conference of the Muslim Students Association of the United States and Canada*, Stanford University, California, 10–12 June 1966, pp. 9–14.

614 'Interest, injustice and Islam – a brief history of money and monetary fraud' (A critique of an interest-based financial system), *Common Sense* (Milton Keynes), No. 2, May 1991, pp. 2–4, 12.

615 AL-KAFF, S.H.A.R., *Does Islam Assign Any Value/Weight to Time Factor in Economic and Financial Transaction?*, Karachi: Islamic Research Academy, 1986.

616 KHAN, Javed Ahmad, 'Muslim dialogue on money, interest and profit-sharing', Research project submitted to Centre of West Asian Studies, Aligarh Muslim University, 1993.

617 KHAN, M. Akram, 'Time is money! Or is it?', *Inquiry*, Vol. 2, No. 2, 1985, pp. 43–6.

618 KHAN, M. Akram, 'Time value of money', in S.G.S. Abod *et al.* (eds.), *An Introduction to Islamic Finance*, Kuala Lumpur: Quill Publishers, 1992, pp. 127–43.

619 KHAN, M. Fahim, 'Time value of money and discounting in an Islamic perspective', *Review of Islamic Economics* (Leicester), Vol. 1, No. 2, 1991, pp. 35–45.

620 MUJAHID, A. Malik, 'Living without interest', *The Message International* (Jamaica, NY), Vol. 16, No. 7, 1992, pp. 23–4.

Riba and Interest

621 ABDEL-BAKI, Muhammad, 'Interest, Riba and Islamic economics', in *Outlines of Islamic Economics*, Indianapolis: Association of Muslim Social Scientists, 1977.
622 ABU SAUD, Muhammad, 'Islamic view of Riba', *Islamic Review* (London), Vol. 45, No. 2, 1957, pp. 9–16.
623 AHMAD, Sheikh Mahmud, 'Semantics of the theory of interest', *Islamic Studies* (Rawalpindi), Vol. 6, No. 2, 1981, pp. 171–96.
624 AHMAD, Sheikh Mahmud, 'Judaism and interest', *Islamic Studies*, No. 20, Spring 1981, pp. 47–82.
625 AHMAD, Ziauddin, 'Thoughts on Riba and interest', *Journal of Islamic Banking and Finance* (Karachi), Vol. 8, No. 2, 1991, pp. 42–5.
626 AHMAD, Ziauddin, 'The theory of Riba', *Islamic Studies*, Vol. 17, No. 4, 1978, pp. 171–85.
627 BEG, M.A.R., 'Interest' (Islamic viewpoint), *Journal of Islamic Banking and Finance* (Karachi), Vol. 6, No. 3, 1989, pp. 44–7.
628 BEWLEY, Abdul Haq, 'The history of usury', in *Usury – The Root Cause of the Injustices of Our Time*, Norwich: People Against Interest Debt (PAID), 1989, pp. 15–24.
629 CHAPRA, M. Umer, 'The nature of Riba in Islam', *Hamdard Islamicus*, Vol. 7, No. 1, 1984, pp. 3–24.
630 CHAPRA, M. Umer, 'The nature of Riba' (Interest), *Journal of Islamic Banking and Finance* (Karachi), Vol. 6, No. 3, 1989, pp. 7–23.
631 CHOUDHURY, M. Alam, 'The doctrine of Riba', *The Journal of Development Studies* (Peshawar), Vol. 11, 1979, pp. 47–68.
632 DOAK, Ervin John, 'Public debt and usury', Paper presented at the Atlantic Society Session, Allied Social Sciences Associations Meeting, New York, 30 December 1988, pp. 1–11.
633 DOAK, Ervin John, 'Interest and usury', Paper presented at the Twenty-Fifth International Atlantic Economic Conference, London, 20 April 1988, pp. 1–21.
634 FARID, Q.M., 'Is interest obsolete?', *Voice of Islam* (Karachi), Vol. 8, No. 10, 1964, pp. 495–502.
635 HABIB, Irfan, 'Usury in medieval India', *Comparative Studies in Society and History*, Vol. 6, 1964.

636 HAQUE, Ziaul, 'The nature of Riba al-Nasia and Riba al-Fadl', *Islamic Studies*, Winter 1982, pp. 19–37.

637 HAQUE, Ziaul, 'Riba and interest', *Journal of Islamic Banking and Finance* (Karachi), Vol. 6, No. 4, 1989, pp. 7–9.

638 'Interest in Islamic Banking', *Inquiry*, Vol. 3, No. 11, 1986, p. 24.

639 KHAN, Javed Ahmad, 'The modern Arab–Islamic thought on interest', M.Phil. dissertation, Centre of West Asian Studies, Aligarh Muslim University, 1987, 142 pp.

640 KHAN, M. Ajmal, 'Islam and usury', *Studies in Islam* (New Delhi), Vol. 1, No. 12, 1964, pp. 86–92.

641 KHUSRU, A.H., 'Usury and interest in Islam', *Newssheet*, Vol. 4, No. 2, 1992, p. 9.

642 MOHTAR, Jamari, 'What is Riba, exactly?' Part 1, *The Muslim Reader* (Singapore), Vol. 8, No. 4, 1989, pp. 2–5.

643 MUSLIM, A.G., *The Early Development of the Islamic Concept of Riba*, Current British Research in Middle Eastern and Islamic Studies, Durham: Centre of Middle Eastern and Islamic Studies, University of Durham, 1971.

644 NEUSNER, Jacob, 'Aristotle's economics and the Mishnah's economics: the matter of wealth and usury', *Journal for the Study of Judaism* (Leiden), Vol. 21, No. 1, 1990, pp. 41–59.

645 NOONAN, John T., *The Scholastic Analysis of Usury*, Cambridge, MA: Harvard University Press, 1957.

646 PARSA, Amir Parviz, 'Riba is prohibited . . . but what constitutes Riba?', *The Message International* (Jamaica, NY), Vol. 13, No. 10, 1990, pp. 27–9.

647 QURESHI, A.I., *Islam and the Theory of Interest*, Lahore: Ashraf, 1974.

648 QURESHI, A.I., 'Views of Islam on interest', *Islamic Review* (London), Vol. 45, No. 7, 1957, pp. 5–10.

649 RAHMAN, Fazlur, 'Riba and interest', *Islamic Studies* (Islamabad), No. 3, 1964, pp. 1–43.

650 SAUD, Mahmud Abu, 'Islamic view of Riba' (Usury and interest), in S.G.S. Abod *et al.*, *An Introduction to Islamic Finance*, Kuala Lumpur: Quill Publishers, 1992, pp. 70–92.

651 ULGENER, F., 'Monetary conditions of economic growth and the Islamic concept of interest', *Islamic Review*, Vol. 55, September 1967, pp. 23–4.

652 *Usury – The Root Cause of the Injustices of Our Time*, Transcripts of a seminar, Norwich, 13 September 1987, Norwich: People Against Interest Debt (PAID), 1989, 69 pp.

653 YUNUS, M., 'Equivalence of usury and interest: an Islamic perspective', *The Message International* (Jamaica, NY), Vol. 16, No. 7, 1992, pp. 21–2.

654 ZAMAN, S.H., 'Islam *vis-à-vis* interest rates', *Islamic Culture* (Hyderabad), Vol. 40, No. 1, 1966, pp. 1–12.

Riba and Its Prohibition

655 CHAPRA, M. Umer, 'The prohibition of Riba in Islam: an evaluation of some objectives', *The American Journal of Islamic Studies*, Vol. 1, No. 2, 1984, pp. 23–40.

656 'Efforts to develop Islamic financial system: focus on the abolition of fixed interest rates', *OPEC Bulletin*, Vol. 13, April 1982, pp. 9–15.

657 HUSSAIN, Zahid, 'Prohibition of interest in an Islamic state', *Pakistan Economist* (Karachi), Vol. 19, No. 46, 1979, pp. 17–21, 26.

658 AL-INANI, Hasan, *The Causes of the Prohibition of Usury and Its Relations of Function of Money*, Cairo: International Association of Islamic Banks, n.d.

659 JAFFERY, Nasim A., 'Ijtihad, Ijma on Riba needed' (Elimination of interest in Pakistan), *Al-Farooq International* (Karachi), Vol. 3, No.12, 1992, pp. 24–5.

660 MAUDOODI, Syed Abul Ala, 'The prohibition of commercial interest in Islam', *Islamic Thought*, Vol. 7, No. 3, 1960.

661 METWALLY, Mukhtar M., 'Towards abolishing the rate of interest in contemporary Islamic societies', *Journal of King Abdul Aziz University: Islamic Economics* (Jeddah), Vol. 2, 1990, pp. 3–23.

662 MOHAMMAD, Omar Bakri, 'Can interest be donated?', *Khilafah Magazine* (London), Vol. 3, No. 5, 1992, pp. 4–6.

663 MONTEFIORE, Hugh, 'Is interest immoral?', *Banking World*, December 1984, pp. 18–19.

664 QADRI, S.M., 'The Quranic approach to the problem of interest in the context of Islamic social system', *Islamic Culture*, Vol. 55, No. 1, pp. 36–47.

665 *Report of the Panel of Economists and Bankers on Elimination of Interest from the Economy*, Islamabad: Council of Islamic Ideology, 1980.

666 *Report of the Workshop on Elimination of Interest from Government Transactions*, Islamabad: International Institute of Islamic Economics, 1984.

667 RUBY, Atiya, 'Prohibition of interest and Islam', *Hamdard Islamicus* (Karachi), Vol. 12, No. 3, 1989, pp. 95–8.

668 SAMIULLAH, Mohammad, *Prohibition of Riba (Interest) and Insurance in the Light of Islam*, Karachi: Siddiqi Trust, 1986.

669 SAMIULLAH, Mohammad, 'Prohibition of Riba (interest) and insurance in the light of Islam', *Islamic Studies*, No. 21, Summer 1982, pp. 53–67.

670 SHARRAF, B.A., 'Abolition of interest in modern banking system', *Arabia* (London), August 1984, pp. 46–7.

671 SIDDIQI, M.A.M., 'Riba – usury and interest: Quran's verdict is clear', *Islamic Order* (Karachi), Vol. 2, No. 2, 1980, pp. 40–70.

Laws for Riba (Interest)

672 AHMAD, Badar Durrez, 'Riba in Islamic law', *Islamic and Comparative Law Quarterly* (New Delhi), Vol. 6, 1986, pp. 51–70.

673 AHMAD, Khurshid, Review article on *Unlawful Gain and Legitimate Profit in Islamic Law: Riba, Gharar and Islamic Banking* by Nabil Saleh, in *The Muslim World Book Review* (Leicester), Vol. 9, No. 3, 1989, pp. 24–30.

674 AHMAD, Syed, 'Reflections on the concept and the law of Riba', in *Outlines of Islamic Economics*, Indianapolis: Association of Muslim Social Scientists, 1977, pp. 26–36.

675 'Are Muslims allowed under Shari'ah to borrow money?', *Khilafah Magazine* (London), Vol. 3, No. 6, 1992, pp. 4–5, 8.

676 BADAR, Gamal Moursi, 'Interest on capital in Islamic law', *American–Arab Affairs* (Washington, DC), No. 29, Summer 1989, pp. 86–95.

677 CHAPRA, M. Umer, 'The nature of Riba and its treatment in the Quran, Hadith and Fiqh', in S.G.S. Abod *et al.* (eds.), *An Introduction to Islamic Finance*, Kuala Lumpur: Quill Publishers, 1992, pp. 33–55.

678 ELGOUSI, Abdelmenem Mahmoud, 'Riba, Islamic law and interest', Ph.D. dissertation, Temple University, 1982.

679 'Interest and the Shariah', *Middle East Economic Digest*, August 1988.

680 JONES, Norman, *God and Moneylenders: Usury and Law in Early Modern England*, Oxford: Blackwell, 1989, 288 pp.

681 KHAN, Mir Siadat Ali, 'The Mohammedan laws against usury and how they are evaded', *Comparative Legislation*, No. 11, 1929, pp. 233–44.

682 KHAN, M.S. Ali, 'Usury and the principles of the Muhammedan law', Ph.D. dissertation, University of Oxford, 1928.

683 MUSLIM, A.G., 'Theory of interest in Islamic law and the effect of the interpretation of this by the Hanafi school up to the end of the Mughal empire', Ph.D. dissertation, University of Glasgow, 1974.

684 AL-QUSI, A.M., 'Riba, Islamic law and interest', Ph.D. dissertation, Temple University, 1982.

Credit and Loan

685 IFTIKHAR, Asif, 'Sheikh Mahmood Ahmad's concept of time multiple counter loan', *Renaissance* (Lahore), Vol. 2, No. 8, 1992, pp. 16–24.

686 KAMALUDDIN, S., 'No interest in lending', *Far Eastern Economic Review*, 30 June 1983, p. 56.

687 LATIF, Muhammad Abdul, 'Is indexation of loans permitted?', in M.A. Huq (ed.), *Thoughts on Islamic Banking*, Dhaka: Islamic Economics Research Bureau, 1982, pp. 112–13.

688 MANNAN, M.A., 'Consumption loans in Islam', *Islamic Review* (London), Vol. 58, No. 3, 1970, pp. 19–22.

689 SHAH, Syed Yaqub, 'Islam and productive credit', *Islamic Review* (London), Vol. 47, No. 3, 1959, pp. 34–37.

690 ZAMAN, Hasanuz S.M, 'Interest-free consumption loans and consumer behaviour', in *Some Economic Aspects of Islam*, Karachi: Mu'tamar-e'-Alam-al Islamis, 1965, pp. 147–62.

Economic Implications of Riba

691 AHMAD, Sheikh Mahmud, 'Interest and unemployment', *Islamic Studies* (Islamabad), Vol. 8, No. 1, 1969, pp. 9–46.

692 AHMAD, Ziauddin, *Report of the Workshop on Elimination of Interest from Government Transactions*, Islamabad: International Institute of Islamic Economics, 1984.

693 BARNES, R.H. and BARNES, Ruth, 'Barter and money in an Indonesian village economy', *Man: The Journal of the Royal Anthropological Institute*, Vol. 24, No. 3, 1989, pp. 399–418.

694 CHAPRA, M. Umer, 'A matter of interest: the rationale of Islam's anti-interest stance', *Ahlan Wa Sahlan* (Saudia inflight magazine), October 1992, pp. 38–41.

695 DOAK, Ervin John, 'Public debt and usury', Paper presented at the Atlantic Society Session, Allied Social Sciences Associations Meeting, New York, 30 December 1988, pp. 1–11.

696 DUTTON, Yasin, 'Usury and its effect on the environment: a local view', in *Usury – The Root Cause of the Injustices of Our Time*, Norwich, People Against Interest Debt (PAID), 1989, pp. 51–7.

697 HAQUE, Ziaul, 'Riba, interest and profit', *Pakistan Economist* (Karachi), Vol. 20, No. 21, 1981, pp. 14–35 and No. 22, 1981, pp. 13–30.

698 HAQUE, Ziaul, *Islam and Feudalism: The Economics of Riba, Interest and Profit*, Lahore: Vanguard, 1985.

699 'Interest, injustice and Islam – a brief history of money and monetary fraud' (A critique of an interest-based financial system), *Common Sense* (Milton Keynes), No. 2, May 1991, pp. 2–4, 12.

700 IRSHAD, Sheikh Ahmad, 'Islamic economy and the elimination of interest', *Voice of Islam* (Karachi), Vol. 12, No. 2, 1983, pp. 78–85.

701 KHAN, Abdul Jabbar, 'Elimination of Riba from the banking system', *Journal of Islamic Banking and Finance* (Karachi), Vol. 1, July–September 1984, pp. 24–44.

702 LAWSON, Ibrahim, 'Economic imperialism', in *Usury – The Root Cause of the Injustices of Our Time*, Norwich: People Against Interest Debt (PAID), 1989, pp. 42–56.

703 MIKAILU, A.S., 'On the prohibition of Riba (interest) and its implications for optimum economic performance', *Hamdard Islamicus* (Islamabad), Vol. 12, No. 1, 1989, pp. 57–65.

704 NAQVI, S.N.H., 'Interest rate and intertemporal allocative efficiency in an Islamic economy', in Mohammad Ariff (ed.), *Monetary and Fiscal Economics of Islam*, Jeddah: International Centre for Research in Islamic Economics, King Abdul Aziz University, 1982, pp. 75–106.

705 NATHAN, Harold C., 'Economic analysis of usury laws', *Journal of Bank Research*, Winter 1980, pp. 200–11.

706 NEUSNER, Jacob, 'Aristotle's economics and the Mishnah's economics: the matter of wealth and usury', *Journal for the Study of Judaism* (Leiden), Vol. 21, No. 1, 1990, pp. 41–59.

707 NISSE, Jason, 'No interest?', *The Banker* (London), October 1987, pp. 135–44.

708 NOORZOY, M. Siddieq, 'Islamic laws on Riba (interest) and their economic implications', *International Journal of Middle East Studies*, Vol. 14, February 1984, pp. 3–17.

709 ORR, Abdulhalim, 'Usury-free and usurious economics compared', in *Usury – The Root Cause of the Injustices of Our Time*, Norwich: People Against Interest Debt (PAID), 1989, pp. 35–41.

710 RAHMAN, Fazlur, 'A study of commercial interest in Islam', *Islamic Thought* (Aligarh), Vol. 5, No. 4–5, 1958, pp. 24–46.

711 *Report of the Council of Islamic Ideology on the Elimination of Interest from the Economy*, Islamabad: Council of Islamic Ideology, 1980.

712 *Report of the Panel of Economists and Bankers on Elimination of Interest from the Economy*, Islamabad: Council of Islamic Ideology, 1980.

713 RUSHDI, A.A., 'Interest rate: a redundant instrument of monetary policy', *Thoughts on Economics* (Dhaka), 1980, pp. 163–80.

714 SHARRAF, B.A., 'Theories and facts about interest rate', *Arabia* (London), May 1984, p. 54.

715 ZAIDI, Nawazish Ali, 'Economic implications of Riba', *Radiance Views Weekly* (Delhi), 10–16 June 1990, p. 11 and 2–8 September 1990, p. 9.

716 ZAIDI, Nawazish Ali, 'Riba: its economic implications', *Journal of Islamic Banking and Finance* (Karachi), Vol. 7, No. 2, 1990, pp. 7–14.

Profit and Profit-Sharing

717 AFTAB, M., 'Profit and loss: a new Islamic concept, *Far Eastern Economic Review*, 27 March 1981, pp. 100–4.

718 GAIANI, A., 'The juridical nature of the modern Qirad', *East and West* (Rome), 1953, pp. 81–6.

719 HASAN, Zubair, 'Determination of profit and loss sharing ratios in interest-free business finance', *Journal of Research in Islamic Economics* (Jeddah), Vol. 3, No. 1, 1985, pp. 13–28.

720 HASAN, Zubair, 'Profit-maximization: secular versus Islamic', in S. Tahir *et al.* (eds.), *Readings in Microeconomics: An Islamic Perspective*, Petaling Jaya: Longman Malaysia, 1992, pp. 239–55.

721 HASAN, Zubair, 'Theory of profit: the Islamic viewpoint', *Journal of Research in Islamic Economics* (Jeddah), Vol. 1, 1983, pp. 1–16.

722 KHAN, Shahrukh Rafi, 'Profit and loss sharing', *Arabia* (London), March 1984, pp. 48–50.

723 KHAN, Shahrukh Rafi, 'Profit and loss sharing: an economic analysis of an Islamic financial system', Ph.D. dissertation, University of Michigan, 1983, 271 pp.

724 KHAN, Shahrukh Rafi, 'Profit and loss sharing as a substitute for interest in Islamic banking', *Saving and Development*, Vol. 11, No. 3, 1987, pp. 317–27.

725 SIDDIQI, Muhammad Nejatullah, *Partnership and Profit-Sharing in Islamic Law*, Leicester: Islamic Foundation, 1985.

726 ZAIDI, Nawazish Ali, 'Profit rates policy for PLS depositors', *Journal of Islamic Banking and Finance*, Vol. 4, No. 4, 1987, pp. 35–46.

11

ISLAMIC FINANCIAL INSTITUTIONS

Definition and Evolution

727 AHMAD, Kamal Ei Din, 'Islamic banking: man's conscience, God's law', *Arabia* (London), Vol. 5, No. 51, 1985, p. 46.

728 AHMAD, Ziauddin, 'Conversion of interest-based banking to Islamic banking', Parts 1 and 2, *New Horizon* (London), No. 9, November 1992, pp. 10–14 and No. 10, December 1992, pp. 14–17.

729 No entry.

730 ARIFF, M. and MANNAN, M.A. (eds.), *Developing a System of Financial Instruments*, Jeddah: Islamic Development Bank, 1990, 284 pp.

731 ASARIA, M. Iqbal, 'Banking with Islam', *Inquiry*, Vol. 2, No. 12, December 1985, pp. 26–31.

732 'A vehicle of equity and social justice', *Pakistan and Gulf Economist*, 22–28 October 1983, pp. 15–16.

733 CARLSON, Terrance, 'Islamic banking and finance', *Arab Banker*, January–February 1985, pp. 24–6.

734 DULEH, Suleiman A., 'The Islamic banking system', *The Muslim World League Journal* (Makkah Al-Mukarramah), Vol. 19, No. 6, 1991, pp. 44–6.

735 'Explaining the Islamic way of banking', *Middle East Economic Digest* (London), Vol. 33, No. 7, 1984.

736 HAMDI, Abdu Rahim, 'Emergence of Islamic banks', *The Message International* (Jamaica, NY), Vol. 16, No. 7, 1992, p. 27.

737 HUSSAIN, A. and HAQUE, M.A., 'Banking in Islam', *Radiance Views Weekly* (Delhi), Vol. 26, No. 34, 1991, p. 4.

738 HUSSAIN, Mohammad Sharif *et al.* (eds.), *Islamic Banking and Insurance*, Proceedings and papers of an international seminar,

Dhaka, Bangladesh, 27 October 1989, Dhaka: Islamic Bank Bangladesh, 1990, 210 pp.

739 'Interest-free banking: misgivings and answers: process of experimentation', *New Horizon* (London), No. 12, February 1993, pp. 10–13.

740 KHAN, M. Fahim, *Comparative Economics of Some Islamic Financing Techniques*, Research Paper No. 12, Jeddah: Islamic Development Bank, 1991, 48 pp.

741 KLEIN, John and HANNADIAN, Farhad, 'A note on interest and banking in Islam', *Saving and Development* (Milan), Vol. 15, No. 4, 1991, pp. 373–84.

742 MANNAN, M.A., Introduction, in M. Ariff and M.A. Mannan (eds.), *Developing a System of Financial Instruments*, Jeddah: Islamic Development Bank, 1990, pp. 15–25.

743 MUHAMMAD, Abdullahi Sheikh, 'The Islamic way of financing and investment' (Interview), *The Muslim World League Journal* (Jeddah), Vol. 19, No. 9, 1992, pp. 47–8.

744 MURSHID, K.A.N., 'The principles and practices of Islamic banking', *BCCI Economic Review*, September 1981.

745 NAJJAR, Ahmad Muhammad Abd Al-Aziz, *One Hundred Questions and One Hundred Answers Concerning Islamic Banks*, Cairo: Islamic Banks International Association, 1980.

746 PARKER, Mushtak, 'Banking philosophies eye one another', *The Middle East*, May 1988, pp. 30–1.

747 PARSA, Amir P., 'A guide to Islamic banking', *The Message International* (Jamaica, NY), Vol. 16, No. 7, 1992, pp. 17–19.

748 'Recommendations adopted in the seminar', in M.S. Hussain *et al.* (eds.), *Islamic Banking and Insurance*, Dhaka: Islamic Bank Bangladesh, 1990, pp. 143–4.

749 RIZAVI, S. Aizaz, 'World of Islam today: towards interestless banking', in A.M. Zaidi (ed.), *The World of Islam Today*, New Delhi: Indian Institute of Applied Political Research, 1990, pp. 343–51.

750 SIDDIQI, M.N., *Banking Without Interest*, Leicester: Islamic Foundation, 1983

751 'The abbreviated infancy of the Islamic banking system', *Arabia* (London), January 1986, pp. 58–9.

752 ZAIDI, Nawazish Ali, 'Interest-free banking and finance in economic paradigm of Islam', *Journal of Islamic Banking and Finance*, Vol. 3, No. 3, 1986, pp. 31–41.

753 ZAIDI, Nawazish Ali, 'Interest-free banking in the economic paradigm of Islam', *Arabia* (London), June 1986, pp. 50–1.

754 ZAIDI, Nawazish Ali, 'Towards Riba-free banking', *Inquiry* (London), Vol. 4, No. 11, 1987, pp. 22–4.

Islamic Banking: Historical

755 GOITEIN, S.D., 'Bankers' accounts from the eleventh century AD', *Journal of the Economic and Social History of the Orient* (Leiden), Vol. 9, Part 1–2, 1966, pp. 28–68.

756 HAQUE, M. Atiqul, 'An outline of Islamic banking: its history and its contrasts with Western banking', *Islamic Quarterly*, Vol. 30, No. 1, 1986, pp. 62–4.

757 HUQ, M. Azizul (ed.), *Readings in Islamic Banking*, Dhaka: Bangladesh Islamic Banker's Association, 1982.

758 IMAMUDDIN, S.M., 'A historical background of modern Islamic banking', in A.M. Zaidi (ed.), *The World of Islam Today*, New Delhi: Indian Institute of Applied Political Research, 1990, pp. 352–5.

759 ISLAM, Zafrul, 'Banking activities in the Abbasid period', *Islam and the Modern Age* (New Delhi), Vol. 10, No. 3, 1989, pp. 259–74.

760 ISLAM, Zafrul, 'Baitul Mal and its banking activities', *Bulletin of Institute of Islamic Studies* (Aligarh), No. 26, 1993, pp. 53–63.

761 SHARIF, M. Raihan, 'Islamic banking: environment, conception and methodology', in M.A. Huq (ed.), *Thoughts on Islamic Banking*, Dhaka: Islamic Economics Research Bureau, 1982, pp. 57–62.

762 SHEHATA, Shawki Ismail, 'Islamic concepts and principles as practised in Islamic banks: an analytical study', Paper submitted to the Institute of Objective Studies, New Delhi, 21–24 July 1989, pp. 1–43.

763 SIDDIQI, M.N., *Partnership and Profit-Sharing in Islamic Law*, Leicester: Islamic Foundation, 1985.

764 UDOVITCH, Abraham L., 'Credit as a means of investment in medieval Islamic trade', *Journal of the American Oriental Society*, Vol. 87, 1967, pp. 260–5.

765 UDOVITCH, Abraham L., *Partnership and Profit in Medieval Islam*, Princeton, NJ: Princeton University Press, 1970.

766 UDOVITCH, Abraham L., 'Bankers without banks: commerce, banking and society in the Islamic world of the Middle Ages', in *The Dawn of Modern Banking*, New Haven, CT: Yale University Press, 1979, pp. 255–73.

767 USHER, Abbo H. Payson, *The History of Deposit Banking in Mediterranean Europe*, Vol. 1, Cambridge, MA: Harvard University Press, 1993.

Islamic Banking: Contemporary

768 ABBAS, B.A., 'Islamic banking theory and practice', *Arabia* (London), Vol. 5, No. 51, 1985, p. 67.

769 ABDULLAH, Ahmad, 'Islamic banking', *Journal of Islamic Banking and Finance*, Vol. 4, No. 1, 1987, pp. 31–56.

770 AL-ABJI, Kawthar Abdul Fattah, 'Developing the responsibility of the auditor to meet the requirements of investment in Islamic banks', *Islam Today* (Rabat), Vol. 7, 1989, pp. 32–50.

771 ABU WAHID, N.M., 'A theoretical justification of Islamic banks', *Islamic Quarterly*, Vol. 30, No. 3, 1986, pp. 192–300.

772 AFZAL, M., 'Islamic banking in a non-Muslim society', in *Outlines of Islamic Economics*, Indianapolis: Association of Muslim Social Scientists, 1977, pp. 121–7.

773 AHMAD, Ausaf, *Development and Problems of Islamic Banks*, Jeddah: Islamic Research and Training Institute, Islamic Development Bank, 1987.

774 AHMAD, Ausaf, *Contemporary Practices of Islamic Financing Techniques*, Jeddah: Islamic Research and Training Institute, Islamic Development Bank, 1993, 74 pp.

775 AHMAD, Mahmood, 'The banker–customer relationship in Islam', *Bangladesh Journal of Political Economy* (Dhaka), Vol. 11, No. 2A, 1991, pp. 157–66.

776 AHMAD, Shaikh Mahmud, *Towards Interest Free Banking*, Lahore: Institute of Islamic Culture, 1989, 144 pp.

777 AHMAD, Sheik Mahmud, 'Banking in Islam', *Muslim News International*, Vol. 8, No. 1, 1969, pp. 5–11.

778 AHMAD, Ziauddin, 'Interest-free banking', *Journal of Islamic Banking and Finance* (Karachi), Vol. 4, No. 1, 1987, pp. 8–30.

779 AHMAD, Ziauddin, 'Islamic banking at the crossroads', *Journal of Islamic Economics* (Kuala Lumpur), Vol. 2, No. 1, 1989, pp. 23–44.

780 AHSAN, A.S.M. Fakhrul, 'Islamic banking in perspective', *Journal of Islamic Banking and Finance* (Karachi), Vol. 7, No. 1, 1990, pp. 39–54.

781 AHSAN, A.S.M. Fakhrul, 'Towards Islamic banking', in M.A. Huq (ed.), *Thoughts on Islamic Banking*, Dhaka: Islamic Economics Research Bureau, 1980, pp. 83–99.

782 AKHTAR, J.R., *The Law and Practice of Interest-Free Banking with Banking Tribunals Ordinance*, Lahore: Mansoor, 1988, 200 pp.

783 ALI, Manzoor, 'Islamic banking and finance in theory and practice', in A. Ahmad and K.R. Awan (eds.), *Lectures on Islamic Economics*, Jeddah: Islamic Development Bank, 1992, pp. 343–64.

784 ALI, Qmar Abdi, 'Trade incentives in Islamic banking', *Journal of Islamic Banking and Finance* (Karachi), Vol. 6, No. 3, 1989, pp. 39–43.

785 ANWAR, Muhammad, 'Reorganization of Islamic banking: a new proposal', *The American Journal of Islamic Social Sciences*, Vol. 4, No. 2, 1987, pp. 295–304.

786 ARIFF, Mohamed, 'Overview' (Of articles), in M. Ariff and M.A. Mannan (eds.), *Developing a System of Financial Instruments*, Jeddah: Islamic Development Bank, 1990, pp. 3–14.

787 ATIQUL HAQUE, M., 'An outline of Islamic banking, its history and its contrast with Western banking', *Islamic Quarterly*, No. 30, 1986, pp. 62–4.

788 ATTIA, G., 'Towards understanding Islamic banking system', *Journal of Islamic Banks*, No. 43, August 1985.

789 ATTIA, G., 'Islamic banks: theory and practice', *Journal of Islamic Banks*, No. 41, April 1985.

790 ATTIA, Gamal El-Din, 'The origins and foundations of Islamic banking and financial principles', in *The Impact and Role of Islamic Banking in International Finance: Issues and Prospects*, A conference of the US–Arab Chamber of Commerce, New York, 28 June 1985.

791 AUTON, B., *A Review of Islamic Financial Institutions: Islamic Banking*, London: Monadnock International, 1984.

792 AYAZ, Babar, 'Islamic banking: island in capitalist ocean', *Dawn, Economic and Business Review* (Karachi), 17 June 1984.

793 BARKATULLAH, A.K., *Islamic Banking: Theory and Practice*, MDDS project, London: City of London Polytechnic, 1985, 37 pp.

794 DARWISH, Ahmad Sani, 'Islamic financial principles: an overview of opportunities and issues', in *The Impact and Role of Islamic Banking in International Finance: Issues and Prospects*, A conference of the US–Arab Chamber of Commerce, New York, 28 June 1985.

795 DOAK, Ervin John, 'Islamic interest-free banking and 100 percent money' (comment), *Staff Papers* (International Monetary Fund, Washington, DC), Vol. 35, 1988, pp. 534–6.

796 FARIDI, F.R., Review article on *Interest-Free Banking* by Muhammad Uzair, in *Journal of Research in Islamic Economics* (Jeddah), Vol. 2, No. 2, 1985, pp. 109–15.

797 FOAAD, A.A., 'Islamic banks and their control', *Journal of Islamic Banks*, No. 41, 1985.

798 AL-GAMMAL, Ghareeb, *Islamic Banks and Finance Houses*, Jeddah: Dar Al-Shurouq, 1978.

799 AL-GAMMAL, M. Abdul Momen, 'The Islamic bank and the prohibition of usury', *Majalla-Azhar* (Cairo), Vol. 49, No. 2, 1977, pp. 10–14.

800 HAMDI, A.R., 'How do Islamic banks work?', *Impact International* (London), 9–22 June 1989, pp. 15–17.

801 HAMDI, A.R., 'Islamic banking: premises and practice', *Impact International* (London), 26 May – 8 June 1989, p. 16.

802 HASSAN, Hussein Hamed, 'Financial intermediation in the framework of Shariah', *Islamic Economics Studies* (Jeddah), Vol. 1, No. 1, 1993, pp. 21–35.

803 HASSANEIN, Medhet, Review article on *Money and Banking in Islam* by Ziauddin Ahmad *et al.*, in *Journal of Research in Islamic Economics* (Jeddah), Vol. 3, No. 1, 1985, pp. 93–9.

804 AL-HAWARY, S., 'Distinctive nature of Islamic banks', Paper 7/4 for First Advance Course in Islamic Banks, Cairo, 29 August–16 September 1981, p. 64.

805 HOMA, Katouzion, Review of *Issues in Islamic Banking* by M.N. Siddiqi, in *International Journal of Middle East Studies*, Vol. 17, 1985, pp. 295–311.

806 HOMOOD, S.H., 'Islamic banking: limited knowledge restrains progress', in *Arab Banking and Finance Handbook*, Bahrain, 1985, p. 102.

807 HUQ, M. Azizul (ed.), *Readings in Islamic Banking*, Dhaka: Bangladesh Islamic Bankers Association, 1982.

808 HUQ, M. Azizul, 'Islamic banking for social justice', in M.A. Huq (ed.), *Thoughts on Islamic Economics*, Dhaka: Islamic Economics Research Bureau, 1982, pp. 20–31.

809 HUSAIN, Irtiza, 'Need for accounting standards for Islamic banks', *Journal of Islamic Banking and Finance*, Vol. 5, No. 1, 1988, pp. 154–9.

810 IQBAL, Z. and MIRAKHOR, A., 'Islamic banking: major issues of transition', *Journal of Islamic Banking and Finance*, Vol. 4, No. 1, 1987, pp. 47–60.

811 IQBAL, Zubayr and MIRAKHOR, Abbas, 'Islamic banking and the appendix', *Al-Tawhid*, Vol. 4, No. 3, 1987, pp. 90–168

812 IRSHAD, S.A., *Interest-Free Banking*, Karachi: Orient Press, n.d., 100 pp.

813 AL-ISLAMI, Massraf Faysal, 'Principles of Islamic banking', *Journal of Islamic Banking and Finance*, Vol. 3, No. 1, 1986, pp. 19–50.

814 'Islamic banking and finance', in *The Middle East and North Africa*, London: Europa Publications, 1987.

815 'Islamic banking: can practice match theory?', *The Middle East* (London), December 1985.

816 'Islamic banking: convert to Islamic economics', *Arabia* (London), October 1983, p. 60.

817 'Islamic finance – an overview', *New Horizon* (London), No. 9, November 1992, p. 8.

818 'Islamic financial system and banking: some theoretical considerations', in John R. Presley (ed.), *Directory of Islamic Financial Institutions*, London: Croom Helm, 1988, pp. 67–77.

819 'Islamic financial system in 1990', *Al-Nahdah*, Vol. 10, No. 1–2, 1990, pp. 10–16.

820 Islamic Research and Training Institute, *Investment Strategy in Islamic Banking: Application, Issues and Problems*, Jeddah: Islamic Research and Training Institute, Islamic Development Bank, 1992, 404 pp.

821 *Journal of Islamic Banking and Finance*, Special issue on the International Association of Islamic Banks, Conference on Islamic Banking, Finance and Trade, Vol. 5, No. 1, 1988, 162 pp.

822 No entry.

823 KAMALI, A.H., 'Banks and loans under Islamic economic order', *Pakistan Economist* (Karachi), Vol. 18, No. 48, 1978, pp. 32–3; Vol. 18, No. 49, 1978, pp. 32–3; Vol. 18, No. 50, 1978, pp. 19–20; Vol. 19, No. 1, 1979, pp. 27–9.

824 KARATASH, Salim Jafer, 'The training of personnel of Islamic banks', in M.A. Huq (ed.), *Thoughts on Islamic Banking*, Dhaka: Islamic Economics Research Bureau, 1982, pp. 184–92.

825 KAZI, A.G.N., 'Islamic banking in perspective', *Journal of Islamic Banking and Finance* (Karachi), Vol. 1, 1984, pp. 7–21.

826 KHAN, Abdul Jabbar, *Commercial Banking Operation in Interest-Free Framework*, Karachi: Habib Bank, n.d.

827 KHAN, A.J., WASSY, M.A. and SIDDIQUI, K.H., *Interest-Free Commercial Banking Framework*, Karachi: Pakistan Banking Council, 1978, 20 + 10 pp., mimeographed.

828 KHAN, A.J., WASSY, M.A. and SIDDIQUI, K.H., *Some Queries and Replies on Interest-Free Banking Framework*, Karachi: Pakistan Banking Council, 1978, 15 pp, mimeographed.

829 KHAN, Azizur Rahman, 'Customer services of commercial banks – Islamic prescriptions for improvement', *Thoughts on Economics* (Dhaka), Vol. 1, No. 1, 1991, pp. 31–9.

830 KHAN, M. Akram, 'Interest-free banking', *Islamic Studies* (Islamabad), Vol. 16, No. 2, 1977.

831 KHAN, M. Akram, 'Interest-free banking: some further questions', *Islamic Education* (Lahore), Vol. 5, No. 1, 1972, pp. 29–47.

832 KHAN, Muhammad Akram, 'Towards interest-free banking' (Review article), *Islamic Studies* (Islamabad), Vol. 29, No. 1, 1990, pp. 99–102.

833 KHAN, Mohsin S., 'Islamic interest-free banking', *Journal of Islamic Banking and Finance*, Vol. 3, No. 4, 1986, pp. 31–53.

834 KHAN, Mohsin S. and MIRAKHOR, Abbas, 'The framework and practice of Islamic banking', *Journal of Islamic Banking and Finance* (Karachi), Vol. 6, No. 1, 1989, pp. 22–32.

835 MANNAN, M.A., Review article on *Issues in Islamic Banking* by M.N. Siddiqi, in *Journal of Research in Islamic Economics* (Jeddah), Vol. 1, No. 1, 1983, pp. 69–72.

836 MANNAN, M.A., 'Islam and trends in modern banking – theory and practice of interest-free banking', *Islamic Review* (London), Vol. 56, No. 11–12, 1968, pp. 5–10 and Vol. 57, No. 1, 1969, pp. 28–33.

837 MIRZA, Yaqub M., 'Building a portfolio: advice for the Muslim investor', *Islamic Horizons* (Plainfield, IN), Vol. 21, No. 1, 1992, pp. 51–4.

838 AL-NAJJAR, Ahmad, 'Problems, successes of Islamic banks', *Arabia* (London), June 1984, p. 46.

839 NIENHAUS, Volker, Review article on *Banking without Interest* by M.N. Siddiqi, *Journal of Research in Islamic Economics* (Jeddah), Vol. 1, No. 2, 1984, pp. 87–93.

840 NIENHAUS, Volker, 'Islamic banks – a short survey', *Islam and the Modern Age* (New Delhi), Vol. 14, No. 1, 1983.

841 NIENHAUS, Volker, 'Profitability of Islamic PLS banks competing with interest banks: problems and prospects', *Journal of Research in Islamic Economics* (Jeddah), Vol. 1, No. 1, 1983, pp. 37–47.

842 NIENHAUS, Volker, 'Islamic economics, finance and banking: theory and practice', *Journal of Islamic Banking and Finance* (Karachi), Vol. 3, No. 2, 1986, pp. 36–54.

843 NOONAN, Thomas S. and MULLINEAUX, Andrew, *International Banking and Financial System: A Comparison*, London: Graham and Trotman, 1987.

844 PERVEZ, Imtiaz A., 'Islamic banking', *Journal of Islamic Banking and Finance* (Karachi), Vol. 8, No. 1, 1991, pp. 17–41.

845 RABOY, M. Ebrahim Sultan, 'Islamic banking in theory and practice', Ph.D. dissertation, University of Exeter, 1988, 460 pp.

846 RAHMAN, Afzalur, *Banking and Insurance*, London: Muslim Schools Trust, 1979.

847 SADEQUE, Muhammad, 'Component of Islamic banking', in M.A. Huq (ed.), *Thoughts on Islamic Banking*, Dhaka: Islamic Economics Research Bureau, 1982, pp. 103–8.

848 SATTAR, S.A., 'Interest-free banking', *Pakistan Management Review* (Karachi), Vol. 15, No. 1, 1974.

849 SCHOTTA, Charles, 'Islamic banking in the US: regulatory issues', in *The Impact and Role of Islamic Banking in International Finance: Issues and Prospects*, A conference of the US–Arab Chamber of Commerce, New York, 28 June 1985.

850 SIDDIQI, M.N., 'Islamic banking: theory and practice', in Mohammad Ariff (ed.), *Islamic Banking in Southeast Asia*, Singapore: Institute of Southeast Asian Studies, 1988, pp. 34–66.

851 SIDDIQI, M.N., 'Banking in an Islamic framework', in *The Muslim World and the Future Economic Order*, London: Islamic Council of Europe, 1979, pp. 101–11.

852 SIDDIQI, M.N., 'Banking in an Islamic framework', *Islam and the Modern Age* (New Delhi), Vol. 8, No. 4, 1977, pp. 5–20.

853 SIDDIQI, M.N., *Rationale of Islamic Banking*, Jeddah: International Centre for Research in Islamic Economics, King Abdul Aziz University, 1981.

854 SIDDIQI, M.N., *Issues in Islamic Banking*, Leicester: Islamic Foundation, 1983.

855 'Supervising the Islamic banks', *Inquiry*, Vol. 2, No. 5, 1985, p. 25.

856 UZAIR, M., *Interest-Free Banking*, Karachi: Royal Book Co., 1978.

857 UZAIR, M., 'Some conceptual and practical aspects of interest-free banking', *Islamic Studies* (Islamabad), Vol. 15, No. 4, 1976, pp. 247–69.

858 WILSON, Rodney, 'Islamic banking and finance', in *The Middle East and North Africa*, 32nd edn., London: Europa Publications, 1992, pp. 180–4.

859 ZAIDI, N.A., 'Islamic banking – putting concepts to work', in *Islamic Banking Instructions*, Karachi: United Bank, 1984, pp. 9–16.

Analyses of Interest-Free Models

860 ABDOULI, Abdelhamid, 'Access to finance and collaterals: Islamic versus Western banking', *Journal of King Abdul Aziz University: Islamic Economics* (Jeddah), Vol. 3, 1991, pp. 57–63.

861 ABDULLAH, S.A., 'Moral issues in investment: Islamic viewpoint', in Ibrahim Sulaiman and Siraj Abdulkarim (eds.), *On the Political Future of Nigeria*, Zaria, Nigeria: Muslim Forum, 1988, pp. 56–60.

862 ADAM, Mohamed Ibrahim M., 'The perceived problems in the utilization of letters of credit: a comparative study', Ph.D. dissertation, University of Aberdeen, 1991, 497 pp.

863 AHMAD, Yusuf, 'Relative significance of various financing techniques of Islamic banking', Paper presented at a workshop on Investment Strategy in Islamic Banking, Amman, 1987, 14 pp.

864 AHMAD, Ziauddin, *Concept and Models of Islamic Banking: An Assessment*, Islamabad: International Institute of Islamic Economics, 1984.

865 ALI, Syed Aftab, 'Risk-bearing and profit-sharing in an Islamic framework: some allocations consideration', in Z. Ahmad *et al.* (eds.), *Fiscal Policy and Resource Allocation in Islam*, Jeddah: International Centre for Research in Islamic Economics, King Abdul Aziz University, 1983, pp. 253–86.

866 ANWAR, Muhammad, Review article on *Towards an Interest-Free Islamic Economic System* by Waqar Masood Khan, in *American Journal of Islamic Social Sciences* (Washington, DC), Vol. 3, No. 1, 1986, pp. 157–60.

867 AL-ARABY, Muhammad Abdullah, 'Contemporary bank transaction and Islamic view thereon', *Islamic Thought* (Aligarh), Vol. 11, No. 3–4, 1967, pp. 10–43.

868 ARIFF, Mohammad and MANNAN, M.A. (eds.), *Developing a System of Financial Instruments*, Jeddah: Islamic Research and Training Institute, Islamic Development Bank, 1986, 284 pp.

869 BASHIR, Abdel-Hameed Mohammad, 'Financial contracts in interest-free Islamic economics: theory and practice', Ph.D. dissertation, University of Wisconsin, Madison, 1990, 133 pp.

870 BASHIR, Abdel-Hameed Mohammad, 'Profit-sharing contracts with moral hazard and adverse selection', *The American Journal of Islamic Social Sciences* (Herndon, VA), Vol. 7, No. 3, 1990, pp. 357–83.

871 BASHIR, Abdel-Hameed M. and DARRAT, Ali F., 'Equity participation contracts and investment: some theoretical and empirical results', *The American Journal of Islamic Social Sciences* (Herndon, VA), Vol. 9, No. 2, 1992, pp. 219–32.

872 BASHIR, B.A., 'Portfolio management of Islamic banks: certainty model', *Journal of Banking and Finance* (Amsterdam), Vol. 7, 1983, pp. 339–54.

873 EL-BDOUR, Radi, 'The profit maximization behaviour of Islamic banks and conventional banks: a comparative study', *The Kashmir Economic Review* (Muzaffarabad, Kashmir), Vol. 3, No. 2, 1986, pp. 21–40.

874 BISHONI, T.R., 'Islamic banking: some unsettled issues of stability and growth', *Journal of Objective Studies* (Aligarh), Vol. 4, No. 1, 1992, pp. 142–51.

875 Butterworth Editorial Staff, *Islamic Banking and Finance*, London: Butterworth, 1986, 149 pp.

876 CHACHI, Abdelkader, 'Islamic banking', Ph.D. dissertation, University College of North Wales, Bangor, 1989, 371 pp.

877 CHAPRA, M. Umer, 'Towards an Islamic financial system', *Journal of Islamic Economics* (Kuala Lumpur), Vol. 1, No. 2, 1988, pp. 1–30.

878 DARRAT, A.F., 'Islamic interest-free banking system: an empirical analysis', in F.R. Faridi (ed.), *Essays in Islamic Economic Analysis*, New Delhi: Genuine Publications and Media, 1991, pp. 203–33.

879 DARRAT, A.F. and SULAIMAN, M.O., 'Islamic banking: an outline of some conceptual and empirical aspects', *Saving and Development* (Milan), Vol. 14, No. 2, 1990, pp. 185–92.

880 GHANNADIAN, Farhad and KLEIN, John I., 'A note on interest and banking in Islam', *Saving and Development* (Milan), Vol. 15, No. 4, 1991, pp. 373–84.

881 HABIBI, Nadir, 'The consequences of Islamic banking in a macro-economic framework', in F.R. Faridi (ed.), *Essays in Islamic Economics Analysis*, New Delhi: Genuine Publications and Media, 1991, pp. 102–47.

882 No entry.
883 HAQUE, Nadeemul and MIRAKHOR, Abbas, *Optimal Profit-Sharing Contracts and Investment in an Interest-Free Islamic Economy*, Working Paper No. 12, Washington, DC: International Monetary Fund, 1986, mimeographed.
884 HARVEY, Nigel, 'Islamic banking', *Arab Banking and Finance*, February 1989, pp. 38–9.
885 HASAN, Tariq, 'Islamic banking: the need for uniform regulation', *Journal of Islamic Banking and Finance* (Karachi), Vol. 8, No. 2, 1991, pp. 15–30.
886 HOMOOD, S.H., *Exchange of Deposits among Islamic Banks*, Working paper presented to the Islamic Development Bank, Jeddah, 1983, mimeographed.
887 HOMOOD, S.H., *Islamic Banking*, London: Arab Information, 1985.
888 International Association of Islamic Banks, *Model Islamic Bank*, Bahamas: Islamic Development Co., 1980, 37 pp.
889 IQBAL, Z. and MIRAKHOR, A., *Islamic Banking*, Occasional Paper No. 49, Washington, DC: International Monetary Fund, 1987.
890 AL-KAFF, Syed Hamed Abdul Rehman, *Organisation of the Credit Operations under the Islamic Banking System*, Karachi: Islamic Research Academy, n.d.
891 KARSTEN, Ingo, 'Islam and financial intermediation', *Staff Papers* (International Monetary Fund, Washington, DC), Vol. 29, March 1982, pp. 108–37.
892 KHAN, M. Akram, 'A good discussion paper on interest-free economy' (Review article), *Impact International* (London), Vol. 14, No. 27, 1986, pp. 18–19.
893 KHAN, M. Fahim, *Comparative Economics of Some Islamic Financing Techniques*, Jeddah: Islamic Research and Training Institute, Islamic Development Bank, 1992, 48 pp.
894 KHAN, M. Fahim, Review article on *Theoretical Studies in Islamic Banking and Finance* ed. by Mohsin S. Khan and Abbas Mirakhor, in *Muslim World Book Review* (Leicester), Vol. 9, No. 3, 1989, pp. 30–4.
895 KHAN, Mohsin S., 'Islamic interest-free banking: a theoretical analysis', *Staff Papers* (International Monetary Fund, Washington, DC), Vol. 33, No. 1, 1986, pp. 1–27.
896 KHAN, Mohsin S. and MIRAKHOR, Abbas (eds.), *Theoretical Studies in Islamic Banking and Finance*, Houston, TX: Book Distribution Center, 1987.

897 KHAN, Shahrukh Rafi, Comments on 'Profitability of Islamic PLS banks competing with interest banks: problems and prospects' by Volker Nienhaus, in *Journal of King Abdul Aziz University: Islamic Economics*, Vol. 1, No. 1, 1989, pp. 119–20.

898 KHAN, Shahrukh Rafi, 'An economical analysis of a PLS model for the financial sector', *The Pakistan Journal of Applied Economics*, Vol. 3, No. 2, 1984.

899 KHAN, Waqar Masood, *Towards an Interest-Free Islamic Economic System*, Leicester: Islamic Foundation, 1985.

900 KOTBY, Hussain E., *Financial Engineering for Islamic Banks: The Option Approach*, Niigata-Ken, Japan: Institute of Middle Eastern Studies, 1990, 217 pp.

901 Kuwait Finance House, 'Reading in the balance sheets of several Islamic banks', *Islamic Banks Magazine*, No. 13, 1980.

902 MANNAN, M.A., 'Islamic perspectives on Islamic banks: an analysis of nine unconventional roles and operational strategies', in M.A. Huq (ed.), *Thoughts on Islamic Banking*, Dhaka: Islamic Economics Research Bureau, 1982.

903 MANNAN, M.A., 'Indexation in an Islamic economy: problems and possibilities', *The Journal of Development Studies*, 1982.

904 MARTAN, Said S., JABASTI, Anwar A.F. and SOFRATE, Abdul Fattah H., 'Islamic *vis-à-vis* traditional banking: a fuzzy set approach', *Journal of Research in Islamic Economics* (Jeddah), Vol. 2, No. 1, 1984, pp. 31–48.

905 MAYER, Ann Elizabeth, Review article on *Issues in Islamic Banking* by M.N. Siddiqi, in *Middle East Studies Association Bulletin*, Vol. 18, No. 2, 1984, pp. 223–4.

906 MIRAKHOR, Abbas, 'Analysis of short-term asset concentration', *Staff Papers* (International Monetary Fund, Washington, DC), October 1987, pp. 1–21.

907 MOHSIN, M., 'A profile of Riba-free banking', in Mohammad Ariff (ed.), *Monetary and Fiscal Economics of Islam*, Jeddah: International Centre for Research in Islamic Economics, King Abdul Aziz University, 1982, pp. 187–208.

908 MOHSIN, M., 'Problems and development of Islamic banks', *Journal of the Rabitah* (Makkah), Vol. 6, No. 7, 1979, pp. 22–7.

909 MUDAWI, A. Yousif, *Islamic Banks: Problems and Prospects*, Khartoum: Faisal Islamic Bank of Sudan, 1984.

910 MUDAWI, Al-Bagkir, 'Islamic medium and long-term finance', *Arabia* (London), July–August 1986.

911 MUDAWI, Al-Bagkir, 'Medium and long-term finance by Islamic financial institutions', *Journal of Islamic Banking and Finance*, Vol. 3, No. 2, 1986, pp. 16–35.

912 AL-NAJJAR, Ahmad, 'Islamic banks: a model and the challenge', in Altaf Gauhar, *The Challenge of Islam*, London: Islamic Council of Europe, 1978, pp. 220–34.

913 NIENHAUS, Volker, 'Islamic banks in national development and international co-operation: a Western view', *Istanbul Benkasi TAS Spring Conference II Istanbul*, Benkasi TAS Economics Research Centre, 1982.

914 NIENHAUS, Volker, *Why Islamic Banks Need Top Management*, Cairo: International Institute of Islamic Banking and Economics, 1981.

915 NIENHAUS, Volker, 'Banking on contract and co-operation', *Arabia* (London), July 1984, pp. 46–7.

916 NIENHAUS, Volker, 'The potential contribution of Islamic banks to the economic development of Muslim countries', in *New Strategy for Development from Below*, Ankara: Union of Chambers and Commodity Exchange of Turkey, 1987, pp. 51–71.

917 NIENHAUS, Volker, 'Islamic banking: microeconomic instruments and macroeconomic implications', *Thoughts on Economics* (Dhaka), Vol. 9, No. 1–2, 1988, pp. 66–86.

918 QURESHI, D.M., 'Investment financing on the basis of share-risk', *Journal of Islamic Banking and Finance* (Karachi), Vol. 2, April–June 1985, pp. 7–12.

919 RAMACHANDRAN, S., 'Banking regulation and Islamic finance', *Economic and Political Weekly* (Bombay), 23–30 December 1989, pp. 2835–40.

920 ROSLY, Sayyid, 'Welfare implications of interest-free bank asset management', *Journal of Islamic Economics* (Petaling Jaya), Vol. 2, No. 2, 1989, pp. 109–18.

921 SAEED, K. Amjad, 'Business finance in Islam', *Investment and Marketing* (Karachi), Vol. 15, No. 7, 1979, pp. 11–15.

922 SATTAR, Zaidi, 'Interest-free banking, profit-sharing and the Islamic macroeconomic system', in F.R. Faridi (ed.), *Essays in Islamic Economic Analysis*, New Delhi: Genuine Publications and Media, 1991, pp. 82–101.

923 SATTAR, Zaidi, 'A dynamic investment model with profit-sharing in an interest-free economy: methodological issues', *The American Journal of Islamic Social Sciences* (Herndon, VA), Vol. 8, No. 1, 1991, pp. 109–28.

924 SHARRAF, B.A., 'Bank capital and non-bank capital in developing economies', *Arabia* (London), June 1984, p. 46.

925 SHIRAZI, H. (ed.), *Islamic Banking*, London: Butterworth, 1990, 104 pp.

926 SIDDIQI, Muhammad Iqbal, *Model of an Islamic Bank*, Lahore: Kazi Publications, 1986, 90 pp.

927 SIDDIQI, M.N. and AHMAD, Ziauddin, Comments on 'Profitability of Islamic PLS banks comparing with interest banks: problems and prospects' by Volker Nienhaus, *Journal of Research in Islamic Economics* (Jeddah), Vol. 1, No. 1, 1983, pp. 63–8.

928 SPIESSBACH, Michael F., 'Principles of Islamic investment: a primer for Western businessmen', *American–Arab Affairs* (Washington, DC), No. 27, 1988, pp. 40–50.

929 TAYLOR, T.W. and EVANS, J.W., 'Islamic banking and the prohibition of usury in Western economic thought', *National Westminster Bank Quarterly Review* (London), November 1987, pp. 15–27.

930 TROLLE-SCHULTZ, Eric, 'Dilemmas of Islamic banks in the West' (Interview), *Arabia* (London), August 1984, pp. 47–9.

931 UZAIR, M., *An Outline of Interestless Banking*, Karachi: Raihan Publications, 1955.

932 ZANGENEH, Hamid and SALAM, Ahmad, 'An analytical model of an Islamic banking firm', in Cyrus Bina and Hamid Zangeneh (eds.), *Modern Capitalism and Islamic Ideology in Iran*, London: Macmillan, 1992.

933 ZINELDIN, Mosud, *The Economics of Money and Banking: A Theoretical and Empirical Study of Islamic Interest-Free Banking*, Stockholm: Almqvist and Wiksell International, 1990.

Alternative Institutions for Non-Interest Financing

934 AHMAD, Khurshid, 'We need a new economic system to deal with financial woes', *The Message International* (Jamaica, NY), Vol. 14, No. 4, 1990, pp. 13–14.

935 AKACEM, Mohammad, 'Islam and the US banking crisis', *The Wall Street Journal*, 9 May 1991.

936 ARSHAD, M.A., 'Islamic banking is a reality', in M.A. Huq (ed.), *Thoughts on Islamic Banking*, Dhaka: Islamic Economics Research Bureau, 1982, pp. 123–6.

937 AYAZ, Babar, 'Islamic banking: island in capitalist ocean', *Dawn, Economic and Business Review* (Karachi), 17 June 1984.

938 COOPER, Roger, 'A calculator in one hand and the Koran in the other', *Euromoney*, November 1981.

939 HOMOOD, S.H., 'Islamic banking and social development', in *The Impact and Role of Islamic Banking in International Finance: Issues and Prospects*, A conference of the US–Arab Chamber of Commerce, New York, 28 June 1985.

940 'How to convert a US bank into an Islamic finance house', *The American Journal of Islamic Finance*, Vol. 11, No. 5, 1991, pp. 5–7.

941 HUDA, Asif, 'The new Islamic bankers', *The Middle East*, March 1982, p. 68.

942 HUQ, M. Azizul, 'Welfare banking', in *Thoughts on Islamic Economics*, Dhaka: Islamic Economics Research Bureau, 1980, pp. 157–62.

943 HUSAIN, A. and HAQUE, M.A., 'Interest-free banking: need of the hour', *Al-Islam* (Dhaka), Vol. 7, No. 3, 1991, pp. 10–16.

944 HUSSAIN, Abdullah, 'Islamic banking: consolidating the vision', *The Muslim World League Journal* (Makkah), November–December 1984, p. 38.

945 HUSSAIN, Muhammad Kayser, 'Prospects of an Islamic banking system at national and international levels', in M.A. Huq (ed.), *Thoughts on Islamic Banking*, Dhaka: Islamic Economics Research Bureau, 1982, pp. 114–17.

946 'Is an Islamic bank a contradiction in terms?', *Euromoney*, April 1979, p. 53.

947 'Islamic banking: a crisis of credibility', *The Middle East* (London), July 1984, p. 10.

948 'Islamic banking: a long way in a short time' (Interview), *The Middle East* (London), September 1988, p. 34.

949 'Islamic Bank International – the real thing?', *Arab Banking and Finance*, February 1984, p. 42.

950 'Islamic Ummah Bank: an alternative approach to banking and development philosophy', *Al-Nahdah Muslim News and Views*, Vol. 7, No. 3, 1987, pp. 35–7

951 ISMAIL, Abdul Halim, 'Should the whole banking system be Islamised?' (Interview), *The Muslim's Reader* (Singapore), Vol. 8, No. 4, 1989, pp. 12–14.

952 MANNAN, M.A., 'A Muslim World Bank: urgent need', *Criterion* (Karachi), Vol. 6, No. 1, 1970, pp. 15–20.

953 AL-NAJJAR, Ahmad, 'Islamic banks: substitute for commercial banks', *Arabia* (London), February 1986, pp. 59–60.

954 NIENHAUS, Volker, 'A Western European looks at Islamic banking', *The Middle East Business and Banking* (Istanbul), December 1982, p. 111.
955 PARKER, Mushtak, 'Islamic banking: expansion and optimism', *New Horizon* (London), No. 362, August 1989, pp. 12–14.
956 PARKER, Mushtak, 'The rise and rise of Islamic banking', *The Middle East*, October 1987, pp. 23–6.
957 SCOH, Oliver, 'Islamic banking: is it here to stay?', *The Banker*, December 1979, pp. 71–5.
958 'Slow but sure: banking on the Islamic way', *Arabia* (London), February 1984, p. 52.
959 'The 1991 National Islamic Convention Leadership Survey on Islamic Finance' (31 August 1991), *The American Journal of Islamic Finance* (Rancho Palos Verdes, CA), Vol. 2, No. 3, 1991, pp. 2–6.
960 'US regulatory changes: an opportunity for Islamic banking', *The American Journal of Islamic Finance* (Rancho Palos Verdes, CA), Vol. 2, No. 1, 1991, pp. 3–6.
961 UZAIR, M., 'Interestless banking: will it be a success?', *Voice of Islam* (Karachi), Vol. 5, No. 12, 1957, pp. 853–9.
961a 'Viability of Islamic banking', *Arabia* (London), October 1986, p. 49.
962 WHOLERS, Scharf T., *The Arab and Islamic Banks: New Business Partners for Developing Countries*, Paris: Development Centre, OECD, 1983.
963 ZAIDI, Nawazish Ali, 'Towards Riba-free banking', *Inquiry*, Vol. 4, No. 11, 1987, pp. 22–4 and No. 12, 1987, pp. 24–5.
964 ZAMAN, M. Raquibuz, *Feasibility of a Muslim Bank and Insurance Company in the US*, Ithaca, NY: n.d., mimeographed.

Developments in Islamic Banking

965 AFTAB, Mohammad, 'Islamic banking is now two years old', *Far Eastern Economic Review*, 26 March 1982, pp. 102–4.
966 AKER, Amier, 'Islamic banking: covering fresh ground', *Inquiry*, Vol. 4, No. 7, 1987, pp. 24–5.
967 AMEER, K.M., 'Progress in Islamic banking', *Pakistan and Gulf Economist*, 22–28 October 1983, pp. 10–14.
968 ASARIA, M. Iqbal, 'Islamic banking makes headway', *Inquiry*, January 1985.
969 COOPER, Roger, 'The success of Islamic banking', *The Muslim World League Journal* (Makkah), Jumada al-Ula 1979, p. 59.

970 CUMMING-BRUCE, Nicholas, 'Islamic banking moves fast', *Euromoney*, July 1983, pp. 142–5.
971 'Economic and financial development of Muslim society', *Al-Nahdah Muslim News and Views*, Vol. 7, No. 4, 1987, pp. 20–2.
972 HAMM, Simon, 'Global Islamic banking in the year 2000', *New Horizon* (London), No. 363, September–October 1989, pp. 32–3.
973 *Islamic Banking: Conference Report* (Of the Middle East Association), London: Monadnock International, 1984.
974 'Islamic banking: Islamic banks prepare for the future', *Arabia*, (London), September 1983, p. 62.
975 'Islamic banking: shifts to a higher gear', *Young Muslim Digest*, November 1992, pp. 29–32.
976 'Islamic banking: the way forward', *Inquiry*, Vol. 4, No. 8, 1987, p. 23.
977 KHAN, Javed Ahmad, 'Islamic banking movement in the Muslim world and its prospects in India', Paper presented at the First All-India Conference on Islamic Economics, Bangalore, India, 27–28 June 1993.
978 KHAN, Mohsin, 'Islamic banking: getting the priorities right', *Banking and Trade*, No. 1, Spring 1987, pp. 44–7.
979 MOORE, Clement Henry, 'Islamic banks and competitive politics in the Arab world and Turkey', *The Middle East Journal* (Bloomington, IN), Vol. 44, No. 2, 1990, pp. 234–55.
980 PATTON, Kieran, 'Islamic bank seeks special recognition', *An-Nahar Arab Report and Memo*, 20 May 1985.
981 ROY, Delwin A., 'Islamic banking', *Middle Eastern Studies* (London), Vol. 27, No. 3, 1991, pp. 427–56.
982 SYEDAIN, Hashi, 'Counting on the Quran', *Management Today* (London), 1989, pp. 104–8.
983 WILSON, Rodney, 'Retail development and wholesale possibilities', in Rodney Wilson (ed.), *Islamic Financial Markets*, London: Routledge, 1990, pp. 7–18.
984 WILSON, Rodney, 'Competition in Islamic banking', in Rodney Wilson (ed.), *Islamic Financial Markets*, London: Routledge, 1990, pp. 19–32.

Co-operation among Islamic Banks

985 AHMAD, Ausaf, Review article on *Arab and Islamic Banks: New Business Partners for Developing Countries* by Scharf Traute

Wholers, in *Journal of Research in Islamic Economics* (Jeddah), Vol. 3, No. 1, 1985, pp. 101–4.

986 ALI, Muazzam (ed.), *Islamic Banks and Strategies of Economic Co-operation*, London: New Century Publishers, 1983.

987 HAMITO-GULLARI, Besir, 'Strategy of Islamic banking order', *Siyasal Bilgiler Fakultesi Dergisi* (Ankara), Vol. 43, No. 1–2, 1988, pp. 19–32.

988 ISLAM, M. Tajul, 'Inter-bank relationship in the case of an Islamic bank', in M.A. Huq (ed.), *Thoughts on Islamic Banking*, Dhaka: Islamic Economics Research Bureau, 1982, pp. 26–30.

989 'Islamic banking: profit from the spirit of co-operation', *Arabia* (London), February 1984, p. 52.

990 'Islamic banking: seminar recommends co-operation', *Inquiry*, Vol. 2, No. 5, 1985, p. 24.

991 KARATASH, S.J. and AL-HANNAWI, M.S., *Islamic Banks: A Challenge for Co-operation*, Jeddah: Islamic Development Bank, 1984, mimeographed.

992 KHAN, M. Fahim, Review article on *Islamic Banks and Strategies for Economic Co-operation* ed. Muazzam Ali, in *Journal of Research in Islamic Economics* (Jeddah), Vol. 2, No. 1, 1984, pp. 63–7.

993 MUDAWI, Bugkir, 'How Islamic banks can aid governments' (Interview), *Arabia* (London), January 1984, pp. 58–9.

994 QASIM, Qasim M., 'Islamic banking: new opportunities for co-operation between Western and Islamic financial institutions', *Journal of Islamic Banking and Finance*, Vol. 3, No. 2, 1986, pp. 55–61.

995 WHOLERS, Scharf T., 'Possible co-operation strategies for Islamic banks', in M. Ali (ed.), *Islamic Banks and Strategies of Economic Co-operation*, London: New Century Publishers, 1982, pp. 40–54.

996 ZAIDI, Nawazish Ali, 'The need and economics of co-operation among Islamic banks', *Journal of Islamic Banking and Finance*, Vol. 5, No. 1, 1988, pp. 145–53.

12

ISLAMIC MONETARY AND FINANCIAL THEORY

Monetary Theory and Policy

997 AHMAD, Khurshid, *Towards a Monetary and Fiscal System of Islam*, Islamabad: Institute of Policy Studies, 1981.

998 AHMAD, Ziauddin, 'Currency notes and loan indexation', *Islamic Studies*, Vol. 28, No. 1, 1989, pp. 39–53.

999 AHMAD, Ziauddin *et al.* (eds.), *Money and Banking in Islam*, Islamabad: Institute of Policy Studies, 1983.

1000 No entry.

1001 AKKAS, Ali, 'Problem of credit creation by commercial banks in the Islamic framework', in M.A. Huq (ed.), *Thoughts on Islamic Banking*, Dhaka: Islamic Economics Research Bureau, 1982, pp. 127–9.

1002 ANWAR, Muhammad, 'Islamic justice in a monetary system: a modest proposal' (Review article on *Towards a Just Monetary System* by M. Umer Chapra), *The American Journal of Islamic Social Sciences*, Vol. 4, No. 1, 1987, pp. 135–9.

1003 ARIFF, M. (ed.), *Monetary and Fiscal Economics of Islam*, Jeddah: International Centre for Research in Islamic Economics, King Abdul Aziz University, 1982.

1004 EL-BADAWI, Mohamed H. and AL-SULTAN, Sultan M., 'Net working capital versus net owner's equity approaches to computing Zakatable amount: a conceptual comparison and application', *The American Journal of Islamic Social Sciences* (Herndon, VA), Vol. 9, No. 1, Spring 1992, pp. 69–85.

1005 BISHONI, T.R., 'Banking regulation and Islamic finance', *Economic and Political Weekly* (Bombay), 1–8 December 1990, p. 2687.

1006 CHAPRA, M. Umer, 'Monetary policy in an Islamic economy', in Z. Ahmad *et al.* (eds.), *Money and Banking in Islam*, Jeddah:

International Centre for Research in Islamic Economics, King Abdul Aziz University, 1983, pp. 27–46.

1007 CHAPRA, M. Umer, *Towards a Just Monetary System: A Discussion of Money, Banking and Monetary Policy in the Light of Islamic Teachings*, Leicester: Islamic Foundation, 1985.

1008 CHAPRA, M. Umer, 'Money and banking in an Islamic economy', in Mohammad Ariff (ed.), *Monetary and Fiscal Economics of Islam*, Jeddah: International Centre for Research in Islamic Economics, King Abdul Aziz University, 1982, pp. 145–76.

1009 CHAPRA, M. Umer, 'Islam and the international debt problem', *Journal of Islamic Studies*, Vol. 3, No. 2, 1992, pp. 214–32.

1010 HAMIDULLAH, M., 'A suggestion for interest-free Islamic monetary fund', *Islamic Review* (London), Vol. 43, No. 6, 1966, pp. 11–12.

1011 AL-JAHRI, Mabid Ali, 'A monetary and financial structure for an interest-free economy: institutions, mechanism and policy', in Z. Ahmad *et al.* (eds.), *Money and Banking in Islam*, Jeddah: International Centre for Research in Islamic Economics, King Abdul Aziz University, 1983, pp. 69–101.

1012 AL-JAHRI, Mabid Ali, 'The relative efficiency of interest-free monetary economics: the Fait money case', in K. Ahmad (ed.), *Studies in Islamic Economics*, Leicester: Islamic Foundation, 1980, pp. 85–118.

1013 KHAN, M. Akram, 'Inflation and the Islamic economy: a closed economy model', in Mohammad Ariff (ed.), *Monetary and Fiscal Economics of Islam*, Jeddah: International Centre for Research in Islamic Economics, King Abdul Aziz University, 1982, pp. 237–68.

1014 KHAN, Mohsin S., 'Principles of monetary theory and policy in an Islamic framework', in A. Ahmad and K.R. Awan (eds.), *Lectures on Islamic Economics*, Jeddah: Islamic Development Bank, 1992, pp. 323–42.

1015 KHAN, Mohsin S. and MIRAKHOR, A., 'The financial system and monetary policy in an Islamic economy', in M.S. Khan and A. Mirakhor (eds.), *Theoretical Studies in Islamic Banking and Finance*, Houston, TX: Book Distribution Center, 1987.

1016 KHAN, Waqar Masood, 'Saving and investment in an interest-free economy', in A. Ahmad and K.R. Awan (eds.), *Lectures on Islamic Economics*, Jeddah: Islamic Development Bank, 1992, pp. 277–88.

1017 LALIWALA, J.I., 'Inflation in Muslim countries: implication for an Islamic economy', in Mohammad Ariff (ed.), *Monetary and Fiscal Economics of Islam*, Jeddah: International Centre for Research in Islamic Economics, King Abdul Aziz University, 1982, pp. 269–86.

1018 LOONEY, Robert E., 'The relative efficiency of monetary and fiscal policy in Saudi Arabia', *Journal of International Development* (Oxford), Vol. 1, No. 3, 1989, pp. 356–72.

1019 MIRAKHOR, Abbas, 'Theory of an Islamic financial system', in A.H. Sadeq (ed.), *Financing Economic Development: Islamic and Mainstream Approaches*, Petaling Jaya: Longman Malaysia, 1992, pp. 142–66.

1020 NIENHAUS, Volker, 'Monetary, social and international economics: some thoughts on Islamic view', *Economics*, Vol. 28, 1983.

1021 RUSHDI, A.A., 'On Islamic monetary policy', in M.A. Huq (ed.), *Thoughts on Islamic Banking*, Dhaka: Islamic Economics Research Bureau, 1982, pp. 130–46.

1022 RUSHDI, Ali Ahmad, 'Interest rate: a redundant instrument of monetary policy', in M.A. Huq (ed.), *Thoughts on Islamic Economics*, Dhaka: Islamic Economics Research Bureau, 1980, pp. 163–80.

1023 SADEQ, A.H.M., 'Islamic perspectives on monetary and fiscal policies and implications for economic development', *International Journal of Islamic and Arabic Studies* (Bloomington, IN), Vol. 5, No. 1, 1988, pp. 1–16.

1024 SIDDIQI, M.N., 'Islamic approach to money banking and monetary policy: a review', in Mohammad Ariff (ed.), *Monetary and Fiscal Economics of Islam*, Jeddah: International Centre for Research in Islamic Economics, King Abdul Aziz University, 1982, pp. 25–38.

1025 SIDDIQUI, Shamim Ahmad, 'Saving, investment and some distributional aspects of a share economy based on Islamic financial principles', Ph.D. dissertation, Temple University, 1989, 180 pp.

1026 ZAMAN, M. Raquibuz, 'Monetary and fiscal policies of an Islamic state: the claims versus the reality', *International Journal of Islamic and Arabic Studies* (Bloomington, IN), Vol. 5, No. 1, 1988, pp. 17–32.

1027 ZINELDIN, Mosud, *The Economics of Money and Banking: A Theoretical and Empirical Study of Islamic Interest-Free Banking*, Stockholm: Almqvist and Wiksell International, 1990.

Monetary Policy in the Classical Period

1028 ABRAHAMIAN, Ervand, Review article on *Islam and Capitalism* by Maxime Rodinson, in *Science and Society* (New York), Vol. 40, 1976, pp. 88–91.

1029 BEWLEY, Asiha, 'The false growth cycle interest in the credit-based economy together with some historical illustration', in *Usury – The Root Cause of the Injustices of Our Time*, Norwich: People Against Interest Debt (PAID), 1989, pp. 51–7.

1030 BOSTOCK, Frances, 'State bank or agent of empire? The Imperial Bank of Persia's loan policy, 1920–23', *Journal of the British Institute of Persian Studies* (London), Vol. 27, 1989, pp. 103–14.

1031 'Early Islamic mint output' (Seminar report at the University of Michigan), *Journal of the Economic and Social History of the Orient* (Leiden), Vol. 9, Part 1–2, 1966, pp. 212–41.

1032 EHRENKREUTZ, Andrew S., 'Byzantine tetartera and Islamic dinars', *Journal of the Economic and Social History of the Orient* (Leiden), Vol. 7, Part 1, 1964, pp. 183–90.

1033 EHRENKREUTZ, Andrew S., *Monetary Change and Economic History in the Medieval Muslim World*, Aldershot: Variorum, 1992, 304 pp.

1034 FARUQUE, Al-Muhammad, 'Jizyah in early Islam: theory and practice', *Islamic Culture* (Hyderabad), Vol. 61, No. 3, 1987, pp. 55–72.

1035 AL-FILL, Najib Abdul Wahab, 'A critical edition of Kitab al-Amwal by Abu Jafar Ahmad Nass Al-Dawudi', Vols. 1 and 2, Ph.D. dissertation, University of Exeter, 1989, 693 pp.

1036 GOITEIN, S.D., 'The exchange rate of gold and silver money in Fatimid and Ayyubid times', *Journal of the Economic and Social History of the Orient* (Leiden), Vol. 8, Part 1, 1965, pp. 1–46.

1037 GRIERSON, Philip, 'The monetary reform of Abd al-Malik', *Journal of the Economic and Social History of the Orient* (Leiden), Vol. 3, Part 1, 1960, pp. 241–64.

1038 HERBERT, Raymond J., 'The coinage of Islamic Spain', *Islamic Studies*, Vol. 30, No. 1–4, 1991, pp. 113–28.

1039 IBRAHIM, Mahmood, *Merchant Capital and Islam*, Austin, TX: University of Texas Press, 1990.

1040 JUYNBOLL, G.H.A., 'The attitude towards gold and silver in early Islam', in Michael Vickers (ed.), *Pots and Pans*, Oxford: Oxford University Press, 1986, pp. 107–16.

1041 LOWE, John D., 'A medieval instance of Gresham's law: the Fatimid monetary system and the decline of bimetallism', *Jusur: The UCLA Journal of Middle Eastern Studies*, Vol. 2, 1986, pp. 1–24.

1042 MALLICK, B.S., *Money, Banking and Trade in Mughal India: Currency, Indigenous Fiscal Practices and the English Trade in Seventeenth-Century Gujarat and Bengal*, Jaipur: Rawat Publications, 1991, 184 pp.

1043 MOOSVI, Shireen, 'The silver influx, money supply, prices and revenue-extraction in Mughal India', *Journal of the Economic and Social History of the Orient* (Leiden), Vol. 30, Part 1, 1987, pp. 47–94.

1044 MORTEL, Richard T., 'Weights and measures in Mecca during the late Ayyubid and Mamluk periods', in R.B. Serjeant and R.L. Bidwell (eds.), *Arabian Studies*, Cambridge: Cambridge University Press, 1990, pp. 177–86.

1045 MUKHERJEE, B.N., 'The weight of Sultan Mahmud's Indian dinars' (Muslim India), *Journal of the Asiatic Society* (Calcutta), Vol. 32, No. 3–4, 1990, pp. 90–1.

1046 NOONAN, Thomas S., 'Early Abbasid mint output', *Journal of the Economic and Social History of the Orient* (Leiden), Vol. 29, Part 2, June 1986, pp. 113–75.

1047 NORDBO, Jan H., 'The first Arabic coinage', *Araby: Nordic Studies on the Arab and Islamic World*, 1986, pp. 20–4.

1048 SHOSHAN, Boaz, 'Exchange rate policies in fifteenth-century Egypt', *Journal of the Economic and Social History of the Orient* (Leiden), Vol. 29, Part 1, 1986, pp. 28–51.

1049 UDOVITCH, Abraham L., 'Labour partnership in early Islamic law', *Journal of the Economic and Social History of the Orient* (Leiden), Vol. 10, Part 1–2, 1967, pp. 64–88.

1050 VENZKE, Margaret L., 'Special use of the tithe as a revenue – raising measure in the Sanjag of Aleppo', *Journal of the Economic and Social History of the Orient* (Leiden), Vol. 29, Part 3, 1986, pp. 239–334.

Central Banking and Monetary Policy

1051 AHMAD, Ausaf, *Instruments of Regulation and Control of Islamic Banks by the Central Bank*, Jeddah: Islamic Research and Training Institute, Islamic Development Bank, 1993, 48 pp.

1052 AKBAR, Mohammad Ali, 'Towards understanding the role of central banking during the transition to the acceptance of

Islamic principles', in M.A. Huq (ed.), *Thoughts on Islamic Banking*, Dhaka: Islamic Economics Research Bureau, 1982, pp. 156–9.

1053 'Alternative tools of supervision by central banks for Islamic banks', *New Horizon* (London), No. 11, January 1993, pp. 12–14.

1054 Central Bank of Islamic Republic of Iran, 'Monetary resources and banking facilities under the law for usury-free banking', *Al-Tawhid*, Vol. 3, No. 4, 1986, pp. 60–77.

1055 RAHMAN, Shah Muhammad Habibur, 'Functions of a central bank', in M.A. Huq (ed.), *Thoughts on Islamic Banking*, Dhaka: Islamic Economics Research Bureau, 1982, pp. 164–7.

1056 UZAIR, M., 'Central banking operation in an interest-free banking system', in Mohammad Ariff (ed.), *Monetary and Fiscal Economics of Islam*, Jeddah: International Centre for Research in Islamic Economics, King Abdul Aziz University, 1982, pp. 213–29.

Capital and Finance in the Muslim World

1057 ABDEEN, A. and SHOOK, D. *The Saudi Financial System*, New York: Wiley, 1984.

1058 'Achievement of economic integration and peaceful settlement of disputes: promotion of Islamic capital investment in Islamic countries' (The Fourth Conference of the Supreme Council of Islamic Affairs, Cairo, 20–27 April 1991), *ISESCO News Letter*, Rajab 1991, pp. 6–7.

1059 BALLANTYNE, W., 'The Arab monetary fund case and Arab international corporation', *Arab Law Quarterly*, Vol. 6, No. 4, 1991, pp. 344–55.

1060 Banker Research Unit (ed.), *Banking Structure and Sources of Finance in the Middle East*, 2nd ed., London: Financial Times Business Publishing, 1980.

1061 BEININ, J., 'Islamic responses to the capitalist penetration of the Middle East', in B.F. Stowasser (ed.), *The Islamic Impulse*, London: Croom Helm and Washington, DC: Center for Contemporary Arab Studies, Georgetown University, 1987, pp. 87–105.

1062 CARIKCI, Emin, *Countertrade Experience and Economic Co-operation among Selected OIC Member Countries*, Background Paper No. 2, Jeddah: Islamic Development Bank, 1991, 91 pp.

1063 GUL, Abdullah, *A Study of the Economic Cooperation Organization (ECO) with Special Reference to Its Institutional Framework and Trade Promotion Activities*, Background Paper No. 8, Jeddah: Islamic Development Bank, 1992, 85 pp.

1064 KHAN, Tariqullah, *Foreign Direct Investment: Overview and Implication for OIC Member Countries*, Background Paper No. 4, Jeddah: Islamic Development Bank, 1991, 64 pp.

1065 NASHASHIBI, H., 'Major developments in the Arab financial intermediation', *OAPEC Bulletin*, Vol. 6, April 1980, pp. 14–16.

1066 NIENHAUS, Volker, *Economic Cooperation and Integration among Islamic Countries: International Framework and Economic Problems*, Jeddah: Islamic Development Bank, 1987, 163 pp.

1067 PARKER, Mushtaq, 'Banking on the Middle East' Special report, *The Middle East*, December 1987, pp. 41–6.

1068 RAHMAN, A.N.M. Azizur, *Survey of the Participation of OIC Member Countries in Various International Monetary Cooperation Arrangements: Problems and Issues*, Background Paper No. 3, Jeddah: Islamic Development Bank, 1991, 60 pp.

1069 SHOKIRY, Abdel Haq, 'Foreign debt crisis and Islamic world', *Risalat al-Jihad* (Malta), No. 73, Summer 1990, pp. 153–61.

1070 *The Theory of Economic Integration and Its Relevance to OIC Member Countries*, Jeddah: Islamic Development Bank, 1986, 82 pp.

1071 WILSON, Rodney, *Recent Financial Trends in the Gulf*, Durham: Centre for Middle Eastern and Islamic Studies, University of Durham, 1981.

1072 WILSON, Rodney, *Banking and Finance in The Arab Middle East*, New York: St Martin's Press, 1983

1073 YOUSRI, Abdul-Rahman, 'Towards positive economic integration among Islamic countries', *Journal of Islamic Banking and Finance*, Vol. 5, No. 1, 1988, pp. 145–53.

1074 ZEINELABDIN, A., 'Inter-governmental capital flows in OIC countries and their determinants: recent experiences and future prospects', *Journal of Economic Co-operation among Islamic Countries* (Ankara), Vol. 10, No. 2, 1989, pp. 55–80.

1075 ZEINELABDIN, A., 'World financial situation and Islamic countries, 1987–1990', *Journal of Economic Co-operation among Islamic Countries* (Ankara), Vol. 11, No. 4, 1990, pp. 49–91.

13

PERFORMANCE OF ISLAMIC BANKS

General

1076 AHMAD, Ausaf, *Development and Problems of Islamic Banks*, Jeddah: Islamic Research and Training Institute, Islamic Development Bank, 1987.

1077 AHMAD, Ausaf, 'Contemporary experiences of Islamic banks: a survey', *Journal of Objective Studies* (Aligarh), Vol. 4, No. 1, 1992, pp. 66–107.

1078 *Arab Banking and Finance*, Bahrain: Falcon Publishing, 1990, 260 pp.

1079 'Al-Baraka expands and contracts', *The Middle East*, March 1988, pp. 40–1.

1080 BASHIR, Abdel-Hameed M. and DARRAT, Ali F., 'Equity participation contracts and investment: some theoretical and empirical results' (Islamic viewpoint), *The American Journal of Islamic Social Sciences* (Herndon, VA), Vol. 9, No. 2, 1992, pp. 219–32.

1081 DARRAT, Ali F., 'The Islamic interest-free banking system: some empirical evidence', *Applied Economics*, 1988, pp. 417–25.

1082 IBRAHIM, Anwar, 'Islamic banking must compete in the financial market place', *New Horizon* (London), No. 395, August–September 1992, pp. 10–11.

1083 International Association of Islamic Banks, *Report on Most Important Achievements of IAIB* (Documents, 1977–80), Cairo: IAIB, n.d., mimeographed.

1084 'Islamic banking: a global success story', *Newsweek*, May 1993.

1085 'Islamic banking: major deals as IAIB opens for universe', *Arabia* (London), March 1983, p. 60.

1086 'Islamic banking operation', in John R. Presley (ed.), *Directory of Islamic Financial Institutions*, London: Croom Helm, 1988, pp. 20–36.

1087 'Islamic banking: poignant lessons', *Inquiry*, Vol. 4, No. 12, 1987, p. 23.

1088 'Islamic banks and financial institutions around the world', in M.S. Hussain *et al.* (eds.), *Islamic Banking and Insurance*, Dhaka: Islamic Bank Bangladesh, 1990, pp. 184–7.

1089 KAMEL, Ibrahim, 'A summary of the day to day working of an existing Islamic bank', in Muazzam Ali (ed.), *Islamic Banks and Strategies of Economic Cooperation*, London: New Century Publishers, 1983.

1090 KHAN, M. Fahim, 'Islamic banking as practised now in the world', in Ziauddin Ahmad *et al.* (eds.), *Money and Banking in Islam*, Islamabad: Institute of Policy Studies, 1983.

1091 MOORE, Clement Henry, 'Islamic banks: financial and political intermediation in Arab countries', *Orient: German Journal for Politics and Economics of the Middle East* (Hamburg), Vol. 29, No. 1, 1988, pp. 45–57.

1092 NASSIEF, Nabil, 'Islamic banking around the world', *Journal of Islamic Banking and Finance*, Vol. 7, No. 1, 1990, pp. 55–64.

1093 RAHMAN, Habib, 'Islamic banking gains ground globally', *Saudi Business*, 3 December 1984, pp. 14–16.

1094 AL-TAMIMI, Younes, 'Experience of Islamic banks in the Middle East', *Journal of Islamic Banking and Finance*, Vol. 3, No. 2, 1986, pp. 63–79.

1095 'The Islamic Investment Company of the Gulf. An introduction', *The Muslim World League Journal* (Makkah), Vol. 19, No. 5, 1991, p. 48.

1096 ZAIDI, Nawazish Ali, 'Performance of banks under a non-interest system', *Journal of Islamic Banking and Finance*, Vol. 8, No. 1, 1991, pp. 42–50.

Islamic Development Bank (IDB)

1097 'Activities and role of IDB in industrial co-operation', *Journal of Economic Co-operation among Islamic Countries* (Ankara), Vol. 8, No. 2, 1987, pp. 27–48.

1098 ALI, A., 'The role of the Islamic Development Bank in the development process of its member countries', *Journal of Economic Co-operation among Islamic Countries* (Ankara), Vol. 10, No. 2, 1989, pp. 1–22.

1099 'Bank analysis: Islamic Development Bank', *Middle East Economic Digest*, 28 April 1989, p. 4.

1100 HAQ, Mohammad Kayed Abdel, 'Islamic Development Bank', *The American Journal of Islamic Finance* (Rancho Palos Verdes, CA), Vol. 2, No. 3, 1991, pp. 7–10.

1101 'IDB: an organisation with little impact on Islamic economic development', *Banking and Trade*, No. 1, Spring 1987, pp. 51–3.

1102 'IDB boosts Islamic trade', *The Middle East*, November 1987, p. 34.

1103 'IDB finances Islamic economics', MEED Special Report, *Arab Banking*, November 1981, pp. 20–3.

1104 'IDB: new routes for development', *The Middle East*, August 1988, p. 29.

1105 'IDB's (Islamic Development Bank) assistance enhances Islamic solidarity', *New Horizon* (London), No. 386, October 1991, pp. 14–15.

1106 'IDB's Unit Investment Fund: objectives, activities and future plan', *Islamic Economic Studies* (Jeddah), Vol. 1, No. 1, 1993, pp. 89–91.

1107 Islamic Development Bank, *Annual Report* (1991–2), Jeddah: Islamic Development Bank, 1992, 216 pp.

1108 Islamic Development Bank, *Survey of the Progress Achieved in the Field of Promotion of Cooperation among the Islamic Banks* (Documents), Jeddah: Islamic Development Bank, 1984.

1109 Islamic Development Bank, *Thirteenth Annual Report* (1987–8), Jeddah: Islamic Development Bank, 1988, 305 pp.

1110 Islamic Development Bank, *Activities and Achievements* (Document), Jeddah: Islamic Development Bank, 1983.

1111 Islamic Development Bank, *Articles of Agreement*, Jeddah: Islamic Development Bank, 1977.

1112 Islamic Development Bank, *Eighth Annual Report*, Jeddah: Islamic Development Bank, 1983.

1113 'Islamic Development Bank', *Arab World File* (Cyprus), 1986.

1114 'Islamic Development Bank', *Arab Banking and Finance*, July 1982, p. 78.

1115 KUHN, W.E., 'The Islamic Development Bank: performance and prospects', *Nebraska Journal of Economics and Business*, Vol. 21, No. 3, pp. 49–63.

1116 MANNAN, M.A., *The Role of Islam in Development with Special Reference to the Islamic Development Bank* (Seminar paper), Niamey: Organization of the Islamic Conference, 1992.

1117 MASOOD, Agha, 'IDB to cooperate with Pakistan more closely', *Pakistan and Gulf Economist*, 22–28 October 1983, pp. 8–9.

1118 QURESHI, D.M., 'Agenda for new strategy of equity financing by the Islamic Development Bank', *Islamic Economic Studies* (Jeddah), Vol. 1, No. 1, 1993, pp. 71–88.

1119 'The Islamic Development Bank: operation, organization, goals', *Middle East Executive Reports*, May 1985, p. 18.

1120 'The role of the Islamic Development Bank: the first ten years', in John R. Presley (ed.), *Directory of Islamic Financial Institutions*, London: Croom Helm, 1988, pp. 49–60.

1121 WILSON, Rodney, 'Saudi Arabia: the Islamic Development Bank's role as a pan-Muslim agency', in Rodney Wilson (ed.), *Islamic Financial Markets*, London: Routledge, 1990, pp. 196–221.

1122 WILSON, Rodney, 'The Islamic Development Bank's role as an aid agency for Muslim countries', *Journal of International Development*, Vol. 1, No. 4, 1989, pp. 444–66.

1123 YALCINTAS, Navzat, 'Credit facilities of the Islamic Development Bank', *Middle East Business and Banking* (Istanbul), July 1982, pp. 18–20.

1124 YOUSEFF, Abdul Rahman, 'The role of the Islamic Development Bank in the transfer of technology', in *Technology Policies for Development and Selected Issues for Action*, Proceedings of a seminar organized by Islamic Development Bank and UNCTAD, Jeddah, 1986, New York: United Nations, 1988, pp. 63–73.

Dar al-Mal al-Islami (DMI)

1125 AKDAG, Sezal, 'The Dar al-Maal al-Islami Trust', *New Middle East*, March 1985, p. 42.

1126 ALI, Qmar Abdi, 'DMI (Dar al-Maal al-Islami) under microscope' (Interview), *New Horizon* (London), No. 362, August 1989, pp. 15–16.

1127 'Dar al-Mal al-Islami Group: important catalyst in Islamic finance', *New Horizon* (London), No. 385, September 1991, pp. 14–16.

1128 'DMI launches solidarity service', *Arabia* (London), January 1984, p. 60.

1129 'DMI looks to the future', *Banking and Trade*, No. 1, Spring 1987, pp. 66-7.

1130 'Islamic banking: how DMI sees its past and global future', *Arabia* (London), February 1983, p. 64.
1131 JENKINS, Lain, 'DMI looks to the future', *Middle East Economic Digest*, 18 January 1985, pp. 12–14.
1132 'Muslim masses support pioneer investment company, Dar al-Maal al-Islami', *New Horizon* (London), No. 362, August 1989, pp. 17–18.
1133 TARBUSH, Susannah, 'Dar al-Mal is poised for rapid expansion', *The Middle East*, March 1982, pp. 50–1.

Individual Countries

Bahrain

1134 'Albaraka Islamic Investment Bank Bahrain', *The American Journal of Islamic Finance* (Rancho Palos Verdes, CA), Vol. 2, No. 3, 1992, pp. 4–7.
1135 'Bahrain Islamic Bank: positively beneficial', *Arabia* (London), April 1984, p. 43.
1136 'Company profile: Faysal Islamic Bank of Bahrain', *The American Journal of Islamic Finance*, Vol. 2, No. 2, 1991, pp. 8–11.
1137 'Profile: Al-Baraka Islamic Investment Bank (AIIB), Bahrain', *The American Journal of Islamic Finance*, Vol. 2, No. 3, 1991, pp. 4–7.
1138 No entry.
1139 'The Faysal Islamic Bank of Bahrain', *The Muslim World League Journal* (Jeddah), Vol. 19, No. 8, 1992, pp. 47–8.

Bangladesh

1140 HUQ, M. Azizul, 'Manpower development for Islamic banking and establishment of regional training and research institute in Dhaka', *Journal of Islamic Banking and Finance* (Karachi), Vol. 7, No. 1, 1990, pp. 10–25.
1141 HUQ, M. Azizul, 'Utilization of financial instruments – a case study of Bangladesh', in M. Ariff and M.A. Mannan (eds.), *Developing a System of Financial Instruments*, Jeddah: Islamic Development Bank, 1990, pp. 207–26.
1142 HUQ, S. Ataul, 'Interest-free banking system: its objectives, constraints and prospects in a poor country like Bangladesh', in M.A. Huq (ed.), *Thoughts on Islamic Banking*, Dhaka: Islamic Economics Research Bureau, 1982, pp. 73–82.

1143 'Islamic banking: Bangladesh countdown to PLS', *Arabia* (London), April 1983, p. 61.
1144 'Profile: Islamic Bank Bangladesh – a model for the poor anywhere', *The American Journal of Islamic Finance*, Vol. 3, No. 1, 1992, pp. 21–7.

Egypt

1145 Arab Republic of Egypt, *The Egyptian Study on the Establishment of the Islamic Banking System*, Cairo, 1972.
1146 AL-ASHKER, Ahmad, 'Egypt: an evaluation of the major Islamic banks', in Rodney Wilson (ed.), *Islamic Financial Markets*, London: Routledge, 1990, pp. 33–58.
1147 EL-ASHKER, A.A., 'Islamic versus Western banks: the case of Egypt', *Arab Banker*, Vol. 6, No. 3, 1986.
1148 'Compromise law mollifies Egyptian investment companies', *Middle East Economic Survey* (London), 13 June 1988, pp. B1–2.
1149 'Egypt's Islamic companies play the game', *Middle East Economic Digest* (London), 17 June 1988, pp. 4–5.
1150 'Faisal Islamic Bank of Egypt: an assessment', *Arabia* (London), Vol. 5, No. 51, 1985, p. 63.
1151 KAZARIAN, Elias, *Finance and Economic Development: Islamic Banking in Egypt*, Lund Economic Studies No. 45, Lund: University of Lund, 1991, 269 pp.
1152 KHAN, Javed A., 'Problems of Islamic investment companies in Egypt', Paper presented at the Centre of West Asian Studies, Aligarh Muslim University, Aligarh, India, 25 October 1990.
1153 MUHAMMAD, Ismail Hassan, 'Utilization of financial instruments – a case study of Egypt', in M. Ariff and M.A. Mannan (eds.), *Developing a System of Financial Instruments*, Jeddah: Islamic Development Bank, 1990, pp. 173–8.
1154 MUSLEHUDDIN, M., 'Islamic banking system: comments on Egyptian study', *Muslim News International* (Karachi), Vol. 11, No. 7, 1973, pp. 25–7.
1155 MUSLEHUDDIN, M., 'Comment upon the Egyptian study on the establishment of the Islamic banking system', *Al-Islam*, Vol. 4, April–June 1973, p. 30.
1156 No entry.
1157 ZUBAIDA, Sami, 'The politics of the Islamic investment companies in Egypt', *British Society for Middle Eastern Studies Bulletin* (Oxford), Vol. 17, No. 2, 1990, pp. 152–61.

India

1158 *Annual Reports of Al-Ameen Islamic Financial and Investment Corporation (India) Limited*, 1990–1.

1159 FAROOQUI, M. Aleemullah, 'Economics of operations of Al-Ameen Islamic Financial and Investment Corporation (India) Limited', M.Phil. dissertation, Osmania University, Hyderabad, 1993.

1160 HABIB, Irfan, 'Banking in Mughal India', in Tapan Raychandhuri (ed.), *Contributions to Indian Economic History*, Vol. 1, Calcutta, 1960.

1161 HASAN, Masood, 'Relevance of Islamic modes of investment to Indian economy', Paper presented at the First All-India Conference on Islamic Economics, Bangalore, India, 27–28 June 1993.

1162 ISLAM, M. Tajul, 'Islamic financial institutions: an Indian experience', *Thoughts on Economics* (Dhaka), Vol. 1, No. 1, 1991, pp. 60–3.

1163 'Islamic banking in India', *Islamic Economics News Bulletin* (Aligarh), Vol. 2, No. 3, 1992, pp. 1, 3.

1164 KHAN, M. Akbar Ali and MAJEED, M.A., 'Lease financing – a major instrument of Islamic banking: a case study of Al-Ameen Islamic Financial and Investment Corporation (India) Limited', *Business Spectrum*, Vol. 2, No. 1, 1991.

1165 KHAN, Rahman K. and CHIDA, A.R., 'Islamic banking – an Indian experience', Paper presented at the International Seminar on Islamic Banking, Bangalore, India, 22–23 August 1987.

1166 KHATKHATAY, M.H., 'Practical problems faced by profit-based Islamic financial institutions in India', Paper presented at the First All-India Conference on Islamic Economics, Bangalore, India, 27–8 June 1993.

1167 MAJEED, M.A., KHAN, M.A.A. and FAROOQUI, M.A., 'Financial services offered under Islamic economic system – a case study of Al-Ameen Islamic Financial and Investment Corporation (India) Limited (AFIC)', *Journal of Objective Studies* (Aligarh), Vol. 4, No. 2, 1992, pp. 84–100.

1168 'Profile: Al-Ameen Financial and Investment Corporation (India) Limited (AFIC): another first-rate model for the upliftment of the poor anywhere', *The American Journal of Islamic Finance*, Vol 3, No. 2, 1992, pp. 4–6.

1169 RAHMATULLAH, 'Problems of interest-free banking in India', *Radiance Views Weekly* (New Delhi), Vol. 27, No. 24, 1992, pp. 53, 127.

1170 RAHMATULLAH, 'Islamic financial institutions in India', *The American Journal of Islamic Finance* (Rancho Palos Verdes, CA), Vol. 2, No. 1, 1991, pp. 7–9.

Iran

1171 AMIN, S.H., 'Banking and finance based on Islamic principles – law and practice in modern Iran', *Islamic and Comparative Law Quarterly* (New Delhi), Vol. 9, No. 1, 1989, pp. 1–32.

1172 ARYAN, Hossien, 'Iran: the impact of Islamization on the financial system', in Rodney Wilson (ed.), *Islamic Financial Markets*, London: Routledge, 1990, pp. 155–70.

1173 Bank Markazi Jomhouri Islami Iran, *The Law for Usury-Free Banking*, Tehran: The Bank, 1983.

1174 Bank Markazi Jomhouri Islami Iran, *A Brief Review of Recent Banking Developments in the Islamic Republic of Iran*, Tehran: The Bank, 1985.

1175 Bank Markazi Jomhouri Islami Iran, *Some Recent Developments in Supervision Arising from the New Banking System in the Islamic Republic of Iran*, Tehran: The Bank, 1984.

1176 Central Bank of Islamic Republic of Iran, 'The impact of the new banking system in Iran on the instruments of monetary and credit policy', *Al-Tawhid*, Vol. 3, No. 4, 1986, pp. 78–89.

1177 'Iran: text of the bill on interest-free banking', *Middle East Economic Digest*, Vol. 28, No. 15, 1984, pp. 57–8.

1178 KHAN, Mohsin and MIRAKHOR, Abbas, 'Islamic banking: experience in the Islamic Republic of Iran and in Pakistan', *Economic Development and Cultural Change* (Chicago), Vol. 38, No. 2, 1990, pp. 353–76.

1179 MAHDAVI, Hossien, 'Islamic banking in Iran – cautious progress', *New Horizon* (London), No. 393, June 1992, pp. 7–9.

1180 MIRAKHOR, Abbas, 'The progress of Islamic banking: the case of Iran and Pakistan', in Chibli Mallat (ed.), *Islamic Law and Finance*, London: Graham and Trotman, 1988.

1181 NURBAKHS, Muhsin, 'The introduction of usury-free banking in Iran', *Al-Tawhid* (Tehran), Vol. 4, No. 4, 1987, pp. 89–96.

1182 'Practical aspects of Islamic commercial banking in Iran', *Journal of Islamic Banking and Finance*, Vol. 3, No. 4, 1986, pp. 56–67.

1183 SINGER, Claude, 'Bankers and mullahs – financial aspects of the Iran–US hostage crisis', *Bankers Magazine*, November–December 1981, pp. 27–34.

1184 'Text of the bill on interest-free banking – a document', *Al-Tawhid* (Tehran), Vol. 1, No. 2, 1984, pp. 166–74.

1185 'The Islamic Republic of Iran. Appendix: Islamic Banking in Iran', in John R. Presley (ed.), *Directory of Islamic Financial Institutions*, London: Croom Helm, 1988, pp. 217–53.

1186 ZAIDI, Nawazish Ali, 'Riba-free banking in Iran', *Journal of Islamic Banking and Finance*, Vol. 3, No. 1, 1986, pp. 70–6.

1187 ZANGENEH, Hamid, 'Islamic banking: theory and practice in Iran', *Comparative Economic Studies*, Vol. 31, No. 3, 1989, pp. 67–84.

Jordan

1188 'Jordan Islamic Bank: significant progress', *Arabia* (London), July 1984, p. 54.

1189 SHALLAH, Ramadan, 'Jordan: the experience of the Jordan Islamic Bank', in Rodney Wilson (ed.), *Islamic Financial Markets*, London: Routledge, 1990, pp. 100–28.

1190 SHALLAH, Ramadan, 'Islamic banking in an interest-based economy: a case study of Jordan', Ph.D. dissertation, University of Durham, 1989, 435 pp.

1191 WILSON, Rodney, 'Islamic banking – the Jordanian experience', in Rodney Wilson (ed.), *Politics and the Economy in Jordan*, London: Routledge, 1991, p. 136.

Kuwait

1192 'Interest-free banking Kuwaiti style', *International Management*, November 1983, pp. 50–3.

1193 'Islamic banking: Kuwait meeting looks to future', *Arabia* (London), May 1983, p. 56.

1194 KABBARA, A.H. Shoukat, 'Islamic banking: a case study of Kuwait', Ph.D. dissertation, Loughborough University of Technology, 1988, 476 pp.

1195 RASHID, Ahmad, 'KFH is banking on Islam', *Euromoney*, August 1984, pp. 170–2.

1196 SEARIGHT, Sarah V., 'KFH finds the going tough', *The Middle East*, May 1985, p. 30.

1197 WILSON, Rodney, 'Kuwait: Islamic banking for a consumer society', in Rodney Wilson (ed.), *Islamic Financial Markets*, London: Routledge, 1990, pp. 129–54.

Malaysia

1198 AHMAD, Syed Waseem, 'Islamic insurance in Malaysia', in M. Ariff (ed.), *The Muslim Private Sector in Southeast Asia*, Pasir Panjang, Singapore: Institute of Southeast Asian Studies, 1991, pp. 188–216.

1199 ANWAR, M., 'The role of Islamic financial institutions in the socio-economic development in Malaysia', *Pakistan Development Review*, Vol. 30, No. 4, 1991, pp. 1131–8.

1200 ARIFF, Mohammad, 'Islamic banking in Malaysia: framework, performance and lessons', *Journal of Islamic Economics* (Petaling Jaya), Vol. 2, No. 2, 1989, pp. 67–78.

1201 AWAL, Noor Aziah Haji Mohd, 'Banking system: legal impediments towards its Islamization in Malaysia', *Journal Perundangan* (Petaling Jaya), Vol. 1, No. 1, 1989, pp. 26–31.

1202 HAQUE, Z., 'The role of Islamic financial institutions in the socio-economic development in Malaysia (Comment)', *Pakistan Development Review*, Vol. 30, No. 4, 1991, pp. 1139–42.

1203 HUQ, M. Azizul, 'Islamic banking in Malaysia', *Thoughts on Economics* (Dhaka), Vol. 7, No. 2, 1986, pp. 1–21.

1204 HUSSEIN, T.S. Jaffar, 'A force to reckon with' (Islamic banking, Malaysia; interview), *New Horizon* (London), No. 394, July 1992, pp. 10–13.

1205 ISMAIL, Abdul Halim, 'Sources and uses of funds – a case study of Bank Islam Malaysia Berhad', in M. Ariff and M.A. Mannan (eds.), *Developing a System of Financial Instruments*, Jeddah: Islamic Development Bank, 1990, pp. 193–206.

1206 ISMAIL, Abdul Halim, 'Bank Islam Malaysia Berhad: principles and operations', in S.G.S. Abod *et al.* (eds.) *An Introduction to Islamic Finance*, Kuala Lumpur: Quill Publishers, 1992, pp. 284–313.

1207 'Major issues of transition in Islamic banking. Appendix A: Islamic banking law in Malaysia', in John R. Presley (ed.), *Directory of Islamic Financial Institutions*, London: Croom Helm, 1988, pp. 298–353.

1208 No entry.

1209 PARKER, Mushtaq, 'Bank Islam Malaysia Berhad (BIMB): a banking bulwark in the making', *New Horizon* (London), No. 394, July 1992, pp. 15–16.

Pakistan

1210 ALKAZAZ, Aziz, 'The Islamization of banking and finance in Pakistan and its effects on savings and investment', *Economics*, Vol. 36, 1987, pp. 61–88.

1211 'An insider's view: Zia's bank Islamization is phoney', *Arabia* (London), September 1984, pp. 48–9.

1212 ANSARI, Javed Akbar, 'Pakistan's economic policy: an Islamic alternative to the fund and the bank', *The Universal Message* (Karachi), Vol. 12, No. 2, 1990, pp. 19–25.

1213 FARUQUI, Jalees Ahmad, 'Pre-requisites and consequences of Islamization of banking in Pakistan', *Journal of Islamic Banking and Finance*, Vol. 3, No. 3, 1986, pp. 43–8.

1214 GIERATHS, Christine, 'Pakistan: main participants and final financial products of Islamization process', in Rodney Wilson (ed.), *Islamic Financial Markets*, London: Routledge, 1990, pp. 171–95.

1215 GIERATHS, Christine, 'Islamizing the financial sector in Pakistan: main participants and final product', in A. Wink (ed.), *Islam, Politics and Society in South Asia*, New Delhi: Manohar, 1991, pp. 55–80.

1216 HARRINGTON, John J., Jr., 'Converting from Western to Islamic banking: Pakistan', *Journal of South Asian and Middle Eastern Studies*, Vol. 12, No. 2, 1988, pp. 3–19.

1217 HASAN, Tariq, 'Interest-free system of banking and finance in Pakistan', *Journal of Islamic Banking and Finance*, Vol. 3, No. 1, 1986, pp. 7–17.

1218 HUQ, M. Azizul, 'Islamization of domestic banking of Pakistan', *Thoughts on Economics* (Dhaka), Vol. 7, No. 3, 1986, pp. 27–54.

1219 'Industrial Development Bank of Pakistan: Review of IDBP operations for the quarter July–September 1985', *Journal of Islamic Banking and Finance*, Vol. 3, No. 1, 1986, pp. 51–9.

1220 'Interest-free Pakistan', *The Middle East*, February 1986, pp. 34–5.

1221 'Islamic banking in Pakistan' (Appendix), in John R. Presley (ed.), *Directory of Islamic Financial Institutions*, London: Croom Helm, 1988, pp. 254–97.

1222 'Islamic banking in Pakistan', *New Horizon*, No. 390, 1992, pp. 5–14.

1223 'Islamic boost to earnings in Pakistan' (Special report), *Middle East Economic Digest*, April 1985.

1224 KHAN, Abdul Hamid, 'Islamization of system in Agricultural Development Bank of Pakistan', *Journal of Islamic Banking and Finance*, Vol. 3, No. 1, 1986, pp. 60–9.

1225 KHAN, Abdul Jabbar, 'Non-interest banking in Pakistan – a case study', in M. Ariff and M.A. Mannan (eds.), *Developing a System of Financial Instruments*, Jeddah: Islamic Development Bank, 1990, pp. 227–44.

1226 KHAN, Abdul Jabbar, *Non-Interest Banking in Pakistan: Concept, Practice and Evaluation*, Karachi: Royal Book Co., 1991, 104 pp.

1227 KHAN, Muhammad Akram, *Islamic Banking in Pakistan*, Lahore: All-Pakistan Islamic Education Congress, 1992, 56 pp.

1228 KHAN, Muhammad Akram, 'Islamic banking in Pakistan', *International Journal of Islamic and Arabic Studies* (Indiana), Vol. 2, No. 2, 1985, pp. 21–34.

1229 KHAN, Shahrukh Rafi, 'The Pakistani experiment with Islamic (profit and loss sharing) banking', *The Banking Development Studies* (Dhaka), Vol. 15, No. 4, 1987, pp. 131–48.

1230 'Pakistan's experiment in Islamic banking', *The Middle East*, June 1984, p. 43.

1231 'Pakistan's road to non-Riba banking', *Arabia* (London), March 1985, p. 59.

1232 'Pakistan – the battle for consensus' (Islamic banking), *New Horizon* (London), No. 393, June 1992, pp. 11–13.

1233 PUROHIT, Navneet Mal, 'Interest-free finance system in Pakistan', Ph.D. dissertation, South Asia Studies Centre, University of Rajasthan, Jaipur, India, 1991.

1234 RIAZ, M., 'All banking to go Islamic in Pakistan', *Inquiry*, November 1984.

1235 'Scholars clash on validity of Mudarabahs in present-day Pakistan', *New Horizon* (London), No. 12, February 1993, pp. 14–15.

1236 SHAHAB, H.V. (ed.), *Interest-Free Banking: Introduction and Operation in Pakistan*, Karachi: Asian Secretarial International and Association of Islamic Banks, 1982.

1237 STOCKHAUSEN, Joachim von, 'Islamization of banking: what does it mean for agricultural financing? – The case of Pakistan', *Law and Politics in Africa, Asia and Latin America*, First quarter 1987, pp. 56–69.

1238 UZAIR, Mohammad, 'Banks and financial institutions: growth pattern in the 1980s' (Pakistani banks after Islamization), *Journal of Islamic Banking and Finance* (Karachi), Vol. 6, No. 4, 1989, pp. 10–18.

1239 ZAIDI, Nawazish Ali, 'Performance of banks under a non-interest system' (Pakistan), *Journal of Islamic Banking and Finance* (Karachi), Vol. 8, No. 1, 1991, pp. 42–50.

1240 ZAIDI, Nawazish Ali, 'Pakistan: restructuring the laws for Islamic banking', *Journal of Islamic Banking and Finance*, Vol. 4, No. 1, 1987, pp. 57–78.

Qatar

1240a 'Profile: Qatar Islamic Bank', *The American Journal of Islamic Finance*, Vol. 3, No. 4, 1993, pp. 4–5.

Saudi Arabia

1241 'A risk of replacing capitalism by capitalism', *Arabia* (London), November 1985, p. 52.

1242 KHAN, Javed Ahmad, 'Feasibility of interest-free banking: experiments in Saudi Arabia and Egypt', Ph.D. dissertation, Centre of West Asian Studies, Aligarh Muslim University, 1988, 320 pp.

1243 'New Al-Rajhi Bank seen as major challenge to Saudi banks', *Middle East Economic Survey* (London), 20 June 1988, pp. B1–2.

1244 'Practical Islamic financial procedures in the kingdom', *Arabia* (London), October 1985, p. 68.

1245 'Al-Rajhi Exchange Company: money changes go hi-tech', *The Middle East*, August 1988, p. 30.

1246 'Saudi banking: the Islamic issue is now being thrust on SAMA', *Euromoney*, June 1982, p. 96.

1247 'Saudi banks turn the corner', *Middle East Economic Digest* (London), 17 June 1988, pp. 18–19.

1248 'Saudi branch battle looms over Al-Rajhi entry', *Arab Banking and Finance*, October 1984, pp. 34–47.

1249 'The time of trial of Islamic multinational', *Arabia* (London), November 1985, p. 59.

1250 WILSON, Peter W., *A Question of Interest: The Paralysis of Saudi Banking*, Boulder, CO: Westview Press, 1991, 296 pp.

1251 WRIGHT, J.W., Jr., Review article on *A Question of Interest: The Paralysis of Saudi Banking* by Peter W. Wilson, in *Middle East Studies Association Bulletin*, Vol. 27, No. 1, 1993, pp. 73–4.

Sudan

1252 AHMAD, Osman, 'Sudan: the role of the Faisal Islamic banks', in Rodney Wilson (ed.), *Islamic Financial Markets*, London: Routledge, 1990, pp. 76–99.

1253 AHMAD, Osman Babikir, 'The contribution of Islamic banking to economic development: the case of the Sudan', Ph.D. dissertation, University of Durham, 1990, 454 pp.

1254 KHALEEFA, Muhammad Uthman, 'Islamic banking in Sudan's rural sector', *Islamic Economic Studies* (Jeddah), Vol. 1, No. 1, 1993, pp. 37–55.

1255 OSMAN, Badawi B., 'A note on the role of the Sudanese Islamic Bank in rural development in Sudan', in *New Strategy for Development from Below*, Ankara: Union of Chambers and Commodity Exchanges of Turkey, 1987, pp. 241–56.

1256 SALAMA, Abdin Ahmed, 'Utilization of financial instruments – a case study of Faisal Bank, Sudan', in M. Ariff and M.A. Mannan (eds.), *Developing a System of Financial Instruments*, Jeddah: Islamic Development Bank, 1990, pp. 179–92.

1257 AL-SAUD, Al-Faisal, 'Faisal Islamic Bank' (Sudan), *Journal of Islamic Banking and Finance* (Karachi), Vol. 7, No. 3, 1990, pp. 7–10.

1258 SHAAELDIN, Elfatih and BROWN, Richard, 'Towards an understanding of Islamic banking in Sudan: the case of the Faisal Islamic Bank', in Tony Barnett and Abbas Abdelkarim (eds.), *Sudan: State, Capital and Transformation*, London: Croom Helm, 1988, pp. 121–40.

1259 'Sudan – testing ground of Islamic banking', *New Horizon* (London), No. 393, June 1992, pp. 16–18.

1260 EI-TAHIR, A.M. and SALIH, I.M., *Islamic Investment Operations and Banking Services: The Case of Faisal Islamic Bank of Sudan*, Sudan: Faisal Islamic Bank.

Turkey

1261 BALDWIN, David, 'Turkey: Islamic banking in a secularist context', in Rodney Wilson (ed.), *Islamic Financial Markets*, London: Routledge, 1990, pp. 33–58.

1262 PARKER, Mushtak, 'Islamic banking: Turkish take to new banks', *The Middle East*, July 1986, p. 25.

1263 TARBUSH, Susannah, 'A Turkish success story for Al-Baraka', *The Middle East*, January 1986, p. 20.

1264 'Turkey's new PLS banking legislation', *Arabia* (London), December 1984, pp. 58–61 and January 1985, p. 56.

1265 UCAR, Mustafa, 'Interest-free banking in Turkey: special finance house', *Islamic Studies*, Vol. 31, No. 2, 1992, pp. 219–34.

United Arab Emirates (UAE)

1266 'Dubai Islamic Bank: investment information', *Arabia* (London), April 1984, p. 43.

1267 'Gulf opts for Islamic financing', *Middle East Economic Digest*, 20 July 1990, p. 14.

1268 PARKER, Mushtak and MARTIN, Josh, 'Gulf banking: ahead of the game', *The Middle East*, July 1991, pp. 35–6.

1269 SAUD, M. Abu, 'Islamic banking: the Dubai case', in *Outlines of Islamic Economics*, Indianapolis: Association of Muslim Social Scientists, 1977, pp. 129–35.

1270 AL-SUWAIDI, Ahmad A. Mohammad, 'The finance of international trade in the Gulf Arab states: a comparative study between the conventional and Islamic banking system with special emphasis on the United Arab Emirates', Ph.D. dissertation, University of Exeter, 1991, 747 pp.

1271 'The Gulf: heartland of Islamic banking', *Arabia* (London), November 1985, pp. 55–58.

1272 'The Islamic Investment Company of the Gulf. An Introduction', *The Muslim World League Journal* (Makkah), Vol. 9, No. 5, 1991, p. 48.

Other Countries

1273 ATTWERGY, Bashir A., DBA, 'The Islamic banking practices: possible acceptance in the USA as perceived by Islamic and US Western bankers', Ph.D. dissertation, Nova University, 1988, 246 pp.

1274 'Al-Baraka: Islamic bank for Tunisia', *Arabia* (London), July 1984, p. 52.

1275 FISHER, Omar, 'The case for Islamic leasing in the USA', *The American Journal of Islamic Finance*, Vol. 4, No. 1, 1993, pp. 4–6.

1276 ISLAM, Ghayurul, 'Islamic bank in Philippines: special law to be promulgated', *Journal of Islamic Banking and Finance* (Karachi), Vol. 6, No. 3, 1989, pp. 61–2.

1277 'Islamic banking: breakthrough in South Africa', *Arabia* (London), June 1983, p. 60.

1278 'Islamic first for Kleinwort', *The Middle East*, April 1986, pp. 24–5.
1279 No entry.
1280 KOROUMA, Mohammad, 'Experience of Islamic banks in West Africa', *Journal of Islamic Banking and Finance* (Karachi), Vol. 6, No. 3, 1989, pp. 48–51.
1281 MARFLEET, Philip, 'Denmark's Islamic bank', *The Middle East*, January 1984, pp. 28–30.
1282 'Profile: Islamic Co-operative Housing Corp. (ICHC) Ltd of Toronto, Canada', *The American Journal of Islamic Finance*, Vol. 3, No. 3, 1992, pp. 3–4.
1283 ROBERTS, John, 'Islamic banking gains US toe hold', *Middle East Economic Digest*, 15 June 1985.
1284 'Summary analysis: 1992 North American Survey for Islamic Finance', *The American Journal of Islamic Finance*, Vol. 3, No. 5, 1993, pp. 5–8.
1285 AL-TAMIMI, Younes, 'An expanding Al-Baraka merits the faith of the Bank of England' (Interview), *Arabia* (London), November 1984, pp. 44–5.
1286 'The first licensed Islamic bank', *Euromoney*, November 1981, pp. 113–21.

14

ISLAMIC FINANCIAL MARKETS

Financial Institutions and Services

1287 ABOD, Sheikh Ghazali Sheikh *et al.* (eds.), *An Introduction to Islamic Finance*, Kuala Lumpur: Quill Publishers, 1992, 411 pp.

1288 ABO-HERBESH, Ahmad Moustafa, 'The practical application of the Islamic rules in business administration: financial accounting', in F.R. Faridi (ed.), *Essays in Islamic Economic Analysis*, New Delhi: Genuine Publications and Media, 1991, pp. 148–76.

1289 AHMAD, Khurshid, Review article on *Islamic Business: Theory and Practice* by Rodney Wilson, in *The Muslim World Book Review*, Vol. 9, No. 3, 1989, pp. 2–3.

1290 AHMAD, Ziauddin, 'The present state of the Islamic finance movement', in *The Impact and the Role of Islamic Banking in International Finance: Issues and Prospects*, A conference of the US–Arab Chamber of Commerce, New York, 28 June 1985.

1291 AIJAZI, Masood, 'MSI (Muslim Saving and Investment Inc.): an experiment in Islamic financing' (California), *The Message International* (Jamaica, NY), Vol. 16, No. 7, 1992, pp. 29–30.

1292 ALAITY, Jihan, 'Islamic financiers tamed', *The Middle East*, October 1988, pp. 33–4.

1293 ALI, A., 'Arab investment companies: types, functions and performance', *Journal of Arab Affairs*, Vol. 11, No. 1, 1992, pp. 34–53.

1294 ALI, A., 'Islamic financing: the answer for the future?', *New Horizon* (London), No. 12, February 1993, p. 2.

1295 EL-ASHKER, A. Abdel-Fattah, *The Islamic Business Enterprise*, Beckenham: Croom Helm, 1987.

1296 BEDDING, James, 'Who trusts the Islamic unit trust?', *The Middle East*, July 1988, pp. 36–7.

1297 BUYUKDNNING, Adnan, 'Housing certificates as an interest-free financing instrument', *The American Journal of Islamic Finance*, Vol. 3, No. 3, 1992, pp. 2–3.

1298 CHOUDHURY, M.A., 'The endogenous theory of money and Islamic capital market', *Journal of Economic Co-operation among Islamic Countries* (Ankara), Vol. 12, No. 3–4, 1991, pp. 75–96.

1299 CIZAKCA, Murat, 'Rise of Islamic banks and the potential for venture capital in the Middle East', in Erol Manisali (ed.), *The Middle East and Eastern Mediterranean: Recent Economic and Political Developments*, Istanbul: Istanbul University and Middle East Business and Banking, 1987, pp. 75–89.

1300 DUALEH, Suleiman A., 'How to apply for Islamic financing', *The Muslim World League Journal* (Jeddah), Vol. 19, No. 7, 1992, pp. 34–6.

1301 EBRAHIM, Shahid, 'Investing in mutual funds', *The American Journal of Islamic Finance*, Vol. 3, No. 6, 1993, pp. 2–4.

1302 EBRAHIM, Shahid and HASAN, Zafar A., 'Mortgage financing for Muslim Americans', *The American Journal of Islamic Social Sciences*, Vol. 10, No. 1, 1993, pp. 72–87.

1303 FIELD, P. and MOORE, A. (eds.), *Arab Financial Market*, London: Euromoney Publications, 1981.

1304 GHAZALI, S.A. Sheikh, QMAR, S.A. Syed and GHAZALI, Aidit H. (eds.), *An Introduction to Islamic Finance*, Kuala Lumpur: Quill Publishers, 1992, 411 pp.

1305 GIBSON, Terrance Carlson, 'Islamic finance services' (Interview), *The American Journal of Islamic Finance* (Rancho Palos Verdes, CA), Vol. 2, No. 5, 1992, pp. 7–9.

1306 HAMID, Adil Abdel-Aziz, 'Financial matters: how to start your own business successfully', in M. Omer Abdel-Hadi (ed.), *Let Us Learn: Issues of Your Concern*, Indianapolis: Islamic Book Services, 1987, pp. 76–87.

1307 HANNAWI, Mohammad, 'Potential Islamic certificate for resources mobilization', in M. Ariff and M.A. Mannan (eds.), *Developing a System of Financial Instruments*, Jeddah: Islamic Development Bank, 1990, pp. 111–36.

1308 HARVEY, Nigel, 'World Islamic finance based on community banks', *Saudi Business*, March 1981.

1309 HASAN, Shabeeh Ul, 'Islamic unit trust', *The American Journal of Islamic Finance*, Vol. 3, No. 6, 1993.

1310 HASAN, Syed Rashidul, 'Islam on marketing', in *Thoughts on Islamic Economics*, Dhaka: Islamic Economics Research Bureau, 1980, pp. 233–6.

1311 HUSSEIN, Tan Sri Datuk Jaffar, 'Facing the challenge of Islamic finance', *Al-Nahdah Muslim News and Views*, Vol. 7, No. 4, 1987, p. 23.

1312 'Islamic economy: investment in Northern Cyprus', *The Muslim World League Journal* (Makkah), Vol. 19, No. 3, 1991, p. 48.

1313 'Islamic leasing gains popularity', *New Horizon* (London), No. 11, January 1993, pp. 16–27.

1314 MANNAN, M.A., *Understanding Islamic Finance: A Study of the Securities in an Islamic Framework*, Jeddah: Islamic Research and Training Institute, Islamic Development Bank, 1993, 113 pp.

1315 MOHSIN, Muhammad, 'Assessment of corporate securities in trust of Islamic investment requirements', in S.G.S. Abod *et al.* (eds.), *An Introduction to Islamic Finance*, Kuala Lumpur: Quill Publishers, 1992, pp. 178–211.

1316 NASHASHIBI, H., 'Challenges confronting Arab banking and Arab capital market', *Arab Gulf Journal*, Vol. 4, Suppl. 2, October 1984, pp. 63–71.

1317 PERVEZ, I., 'Islamic finance', *Arab Law Quarterly* (London), Vol. 5, No. 4, 1990, pp. 259–81.

1318 SABBAGH, Hashem, 'The mechanisms and operations of an Islamic financial market', in M. Ariff and M.A. Mannan (eds.), *Developing a System of Financial Instruments*, Jeddah: Islamic Development Bank, 1990, pp. 153–70.

1319 SAID, 'Mutual funds: an Islamic overview', *The American Journal of Islamic Finance*, Vol. 3, No. 6, 1993, pp. 5–6.

1320 SEARCY, Raya, 'Interest-free real estate', *The Message International* (Jamaica, NY), Vol. 16, No. 6, 1992, pp. 31–2.

1321 SEZNEC, Jean-François, *The Financial Markets of the Arabian Gulf*, Beckenham: Croom Helm, 1987.

1322 SHAMZ, M.M.A. (ed.), *Middle East Financial Directory*, Gants Hill, UK: MEFD Publishing Co., 1990, 256 pp.

1323 'The 1991 National Islamic Convention Leadership Survey on Islamic Finance', *The American Journal of Islamic Finance*, Vol. 2, No. 3, 1991.

1324 WILSON, Rodney (ed.), *Islamic Financial Markets*, London: Routledge, 1990.

1325 WILSON, Rodney, 'Islamic financial instruments', *Arab Law Quarterly* (London), Vol. 6, No. 2, 1991, pp. 205–14.

1326 WILSON, Rodney, 'The role of Islamic banks in financial markets', *Arab Gulf Journal*, Vol. 4, Suppl. 2, October 1984, pp. 53–61.

1327 WRIGHT, P., 'Doing business in Islamic markets', *Harvard Business Review*, January–February 1981.

1328 ZAMAN, Ashrafuz, 'Leasing in Islamic finance', *The American Journal of Islamic Finance*, Vol. 4, No. 1, 1993, pp. 3–4.

1329 ZAMAN, Hasanuz, 'Limited liability of shareholder: an Islamic perspective', *Islamic Studies* (Islamabad), Vol. 28, No. 4, 1989, pp. 353–62.

1330 ZUBERI, Khalique, 'Islamic trade financing facility', *Journal of Islamic Banking and Finance*, Vol. 3, No. 3, 1986, pp. 17–32.

Stock Exchange and Securities

1331 CHAPRA, M. Umer, Comments on 'Role of the stock exchange in an Islamic economy' by Mukhtar M. Metwally, in *Journal of Research in Islamic Economics* (Jeddah), Vol. 3, No. 1, 1985, pp. 75–81.

1332 EBRAHIM, Mohammad M. Shahid, 'Are shares and share traders Islamically permissible?', *The American Journal of Islamic Finance*, Vol. 2, No. 3, 1991, pp. 2–3.

1333 EBRAHIM, Muhammad S., 'Commodity exchange and stock exchange in an Islamic economy' (Comments), *The American Journal of Islamic Social Sciences* (Herndon, VA), Vol. 9, No. 2, 1992, pp. 284–7.

1334 ELGARI, Bin Eid Mohammad, 'Towards an Islamic stock market', *Journal of Objective Studies* (Aligarh), Vol. 3, No. 2, July 1991, pp. 22–38.

1335 ELGARI, Mohammed Ali, 'Towards an Islamic stock market', *Islamic Economic Studies* (Jeddah), Vol. 1, No. 1, 1993, pp. 1–20.

1336 HARDIE, Alexander R. and ROBOY, A., 'Risk, piety and the Islamic investor', *British Journal of Middle Eastern Studies* (Exeter), Vol. 18, No. 1, 1991, pp. 52–66.

1337 'Islamic Co-operative Housing Corp.' (Interview), *The American Journal of Islamic Finance*, Vol. 3, No. 3, 1992, pp. 5–7.

1338 KHAN, Muhammad Akram, 'Commodity exchange and stock exchange in an Islamic economy', *The American Journal of Islamic Social Sciences*, Vol. 5, No. 1, 1988, pp. 91–114.

1339 KHAN, Muhammad Akram, 'Taking stock', *Inquiry* (London), April 1988, pp. 28–30.

1340 QURESHI, D.M., 'Islamic instruments of finance: the role of the stock exchange', *Journal of Islamic Banking and Finance*, Vol. 5, No. 1, 1988, pp. 79–82.

1341 SHAHABUDDIN, Syed A. Jabbar Bin, Comments on Muhammad Akram Khan's 'Commodity exchange and stock exchange in an Islamic economy', in *Journal of Islamic Economics* (Kuala Lumpur), Vol. 1, No. 2, 1988, pp. 71–6.

1342 'The Resolution Trust Corp.: opportunities for Muslim investors and innovators', *The American Journal of Islamic Finance*, Vol. 2, No. 5, 1992, pp. 2–5.

1343 ZAMAN, M. Raquibuz, 'The operation of the modern financial markets for stocks and bonds and its relevance to an Islamic economy', *The American Journal of Islamic Social Sciences*, Vol. 3, No. 1, 1986, pp. 125–40.

Islamic Modes of Finance

1344 HAMOUD, Sami, 'Utilization of funds generated through Islamic financial instruments', in M. Ariff and M.A. Mannan (eds.), *Developing a System of Financial Instruments*, Jeddah: Islamic Development Bank, 1990, pp. 137–52.

1345 HANNAWI, Mohamed, 'Potential Islamic certificate for resources mobilization', *Islamic Economic Studies* (Jeddah), Vol. 1, No. 1, 1993, pp. 57–69.

1346 HASAN, Abdullah Alwi Bin Haji, 'Al-Mudarabah (dormant partnership) and its identical Islamic partnerships in early Islam', *Hamdard Islamicus* (Islamabad), Vol. 12, No. 2, 1989, pp. 11–38.

1347 HASAN, Tariq, 'Legal process for establishing rules for Murabaha contracts', *Journal of Islamic Banking and Finance*, Vol. 4, 1987.

1348 HJARPE, J., 'Mudaraba banking and Takaful insurance: the question of Islamic banks: their significance and possible impact', *Proceedings of the ERSA Symposium Week, 1985*, Stockholm: Centre for Pacific Asia Studies, University of Stockholm, 1986, pp. 333–54.

1349 AL-KAFF, S.H.A.R., *Al-Murabaha in Theory and Practice*, Karachi: Islamic Research Academy, 1986, 75 pp.

1350 KARIM, Rifaat Ahmad Abdel and ALI, Amal Ei-Tigani, 'Towards an understanding of the use of financing mechanisms of the Islamic banks', *Arab Journal of the Social Sciences* (Cambridge), Vol. 22, No. 3, 1990, pp. 375–6.

1351 LUAY, Allami, 'Leasing – an Islamic instrument', in Butterworth Editorial Staff (ed.), *Islamic Banking and Finance*, London: Butterworth, 1986.

1352 MAN, Zakariya, 'Islamic banking: prospects for Mudharabah and Musharakah financing', in A.H.M. Sadeq *et al.* (eds.), *Development and Finance in Islam*, Selangor: International Islamic University Press, 1991, pp. 239–52.

1353 MANNAN, M.A., 'An appraisal of existing financial instruments and market operation from Islamic perspectives', in M. Ariff and M.A. Mannan (eds.), *Developing a System of Financial Instruments*, Jeddah: Islamic Development Bank, 1990, pp. 75–110.

1354 MEMON, Noor Ahmad, 'Leasing – a flexible mode of financing (Islamic banking)', *Journal of Islamic Banking and Finance* (Karachi), Vol. 6, No. 1, 1989, pp. 18–21.

1355 MIKAILU, A.S., 'A note on the implications of Mudarabah for capital budgeting decisions', *Hamdard Islamicus*, Vol. 14, No. 3, 1991, pp. 71–5.

1356 MOHSIN, M., *Assessment of Corporate Securities in Terms of Islamic Investment Requirements*, Research Series in English No. 16, Jeddah: International Centre for Research in Islamic Economics, King Abdul Aziz University, 1983.

1357 PATEL, M. Adam, *Mudarabah*, Karachi: Pakistan Law House, 1981.

1358 QURESHI, D.M., 'The role of Shariah-based financial instruments in a Muslim country', in M. Ariff and M.A. Mannan (eds.), *Developing a System of Financial Instruments*, Jeddah: Islamic Development Bank, 1990, pp. 49–74.

1359 QURESHI, D.M., 'Lease financing (Islamic banking)', *Journal of Islamic Banking and Finance* (Karachi), Vol. 6, No. 1, 1989, pp. 33–44.

1360 SARKER, Abdul Awal, 'Mode of Islamic investment: Mudaraba bond', *Thoughts on Economics* (Dhaka), Vol. 1, No. 1, 1991.

1361 SIDDIQI, M. Nejatullah, 'Some economic aspects of Mudharabah', *Review of Islamic Economics* (Leicester), Vol. 1, No. 2, 1991, pp. 21–33.

1362 SIDDIQUI, Shamim Ahmad and FARDMANESH, Mohsen, 'Saving and investment under Mudarabah finance', *Review of Islamic Economics* (Leicester), Vol. 2, No. 1, 1992, pp. 31–51.

1363 'What is Murabaha? An analysis of some modern trade finance concepts in light of the Shariah', *The American Journal of Islamic Finance*, Vol. 3, No. 4, 1993, pp. 2–3.

Insurance in Islam

1364 ALI, Kazi Mohammad Mortuza, 'Islamic insurance', in M.S. Hussain *et al.* (eds.), *Islamic Banking and Insurance*, Dhaka: Islami Bank Bangladesh, 1990, pp. 180–3.

1365 ALI, K.M. Mortuza, 'Insurance in Islam', *Thoughts on Economics* (Dhaka), Vol. 7, No. 4, 1986, pp. 1–37.

1365a 'A model structure of an Islamic reinsurance company', *Thoughts on Economics* (Dhaka), Vol. 7, No. 4, 1986, pp. 81–5.

1366 'A practical application of the Islamic co-operative insurance principles', *Thoughts on Economics* (Dhaka), Vol. 7, No. 4, 1986, pp. 86–90.

1367 FARRUKH, Omar, 'Banking and insurance in relation to the Islamic concept of Riba', in M.A. Khan (ed.), *International Islamic Conference*, Islamabad, 1970, pp. 123–9.

1368 HUQ, Begum Ismat Ara, 'Conventional insurance and Islamic insurance – a comparative analysis', *Thoughts on Economics* (Dhaka), Vol. 1, No. 263, 1991, pp. 47–65.

1369 'Insurance – do we need any alternatives?', *The Muslim Reader*, Vol. 7, No. 2, 1987, pp. 6–9.

1370 'Islamic insurance and reinsurance: a few questions and answers from Shariah experts', *Thoughts on Economics* (Dhaka), Vol. 7, No. 4, 1986, pp. 75–80.

1371 'Islamic insurance comes to town', *Inquiry*, Vol. 2, No. 5, 1985, p. 24.

1372 'Islamic Takaful companies in operation', *Thoughts on Economics* (Dhaka), Vol. 7, No. 4, 1986, pp. 62–74.

1373 KLINGMULLER, E., 'The concept and development of Insurance in Islamic countries', *Islamic Culture* (Hyderabad), Vol. 43, 1969, pp. 27–37.

1374 MANKABANDY, S., 'Insurance and Islamic law', *International Contract Law and Finance Review*, No. 1, 1980, pp. 455–8.

1375 No entry.

1376 MUSLEHUDDIN, M., *Insurance and Islamic Law*, London: School of Oriental and African Studies, 1966.

1377 RISPLER-CHAIM, Vardit, 'Insurance and semi-insurance transactions in Islamic history until the nineteenth century', *Journal of the Economic and Social History of the Orient* (Leiden), Vol. 34, No. 2, 1991, pp. 142–58.

1378 SIDDIQI, M.N., *Insurance in an Islamic Economy*, Leicester: Islamic Foundation, 1985.

1379 'The Islamic Insurance Company Ltd Sudan: structure and operation' (Case study), *Thoughts on Economics* (Dhaka), Vol. 7, No. 4, 1986, pp. 75–80.

1380 YOUSOF, Mohammad Fadzli, 'Takaful: an Islamic alternative to insurance', in M.S. Hussain *et al.* (eds.), *Islamic Banking and Insurance*, Dhaka: Islami Bank Bangladesh, 1990, pp. 61–77.

1380a YOUSOF, Mohammad Fadzli, 'Takaful: an Islamic alternative to insurance', *Journal of Islamic Banking and Finance*, Vol. 7, No. 1, 1990, pp. 39–54.

1381 ZAMAN, Requibuz, 'Some issues in risk management and insurance in a non-Muslim state', in F.R. Faridi (ed.), *Essays in Islamic Economic Analysis*, New Delhi: Genuine Publications and Media, 1991, pp. 224–36.

Islamic Common Market

1382 ALATAS, Syed Farid, 'An Islamic common market and economic development', *Islamic Culture*, Vol. 61, No. 1, 1987, pp. 28–38.

1383 CINDORUK, Sadi, 'International economic integration and prospects for an Islamic common market', *Journal of Islamic Banking and Finance*, Vol. 5, No. 1, 1988, pp. 113–18.

1384 HAQQI, Muhammad Ali, 'The Islamic countries common market: a necessity despite hindrance', *Echo of Islam* (Tehran), No. 97, July 1992, pp. 50–3.

1385 MDAGHRI, Driss Alaoni, 'Towards an Islamic common market', *Journal of Islamic Banking and Finance*, Vol. 5, No. 1, 1988, pp. 73–8.

1386 NASSER, El-Gharib, 'The role of Islamic banks for initiating an Islamic common market', *Journal of Islamic Banking and Finance*, Vol. 5, No. 1, 1988, pp. 119–38.

1387 PIRZADA, Syed Sharifuddin, 'Islamic common market: a personal view' (Interview), *Banking and Trade*, No. 1, Spring 1987, pp. 9–10.

1388 SHALABY, Ismail, 'The Islamic common market', *Journal of Islamic Banking and Finance*, Vol. 5, No. 1, 1988, pp. 83–112.

1389 ZAMAN, Ashrufuz, 'A practical project for the implementation of Islamic common market', *Journal of Islamic Banking and Finance*, Vol. 5, No. 1, 1988, pp. 139–44.

15

ISLAMIC FISCAL POLICY AND PUBLIC FINANCE

Taxation in Islam

1390 AHMAD, Ziauddin (ed.), *Fiscal Policy and Resource Allocation in Islam*, Islamabad: Institute of Policy Studies, 1983.

1391 AHMAD, Ziauddin, 'Public finance and fiscal policy in an Islamic perspective', in A. Ahmad and K.R. Awan (eds.), *Lectures on Islamic Economics*, Jeddah: Islamic Development Bank, 1992, pp. 365–94.

1392 ATHAMINA, Khalil, 'Taxation reforms in early Islamic Khurasan: a reassessment', *Der Islam*, Vol. 65, No. 4, 1988, pp. 272–81.

1393 AWAD, Mohammad H., 'Adjusting tax structure to accommodate Zakah', in I.A. Imtiazi *et al.* (eds.), *Management of Zakah in Modern Muslim Society*, Jeddah: Islamic Research and Training Institute, Islamic Development Bank, 1989, pp. 77–96.

1394 CHAPRA, M. Umer, 'Reforming the public finance in Muslim countries to realize growth with equity', in A.H.M. Sadeq (ed.), *Financing Economic Development: Islamic and Mainstream Approaches*, Petaling Jaya: Longman Malaysia, 1992, pp. 125–41.

1395 DARLING, Linda T., 'Ottoman salary registers as a source for economic and social history', *The Turkish Studies Association Bulletin* (Muncie, IN), Vol. 14, No. 1, 1990, pp. 13–34.

1396 FARIDI, F.R., 'The Islamic criteria of the distribution of tax burden', *Journal of Objective Studies* (Aligarh), Vol. 4, No. 1, 1992, pp. 1–13.

1397 FARIDI, F.R., 'Capital formation, economic growth and public budgeting in an Islamic framework', in A.H.M. Sadeq (ed.), *Financing Economic Development: Islamic and Mainstream*

Approaches, Petaling Jaya: Longman Malaysia, 1992, pp. 96–124.

1398 AL-FILL, Najib Abdul Wahab, 'A critical edition of Kitab al-Amwal by Abu Jafar Ahmad Nass Al-Dawudi', Vols. 1 and 2, Ph.D. dissertation, University of Exeter, 1989, 693 pp.

1399 GLICK, Thomas F., 'Muhtasib and Mustasaf: a case study of institutional diffusion', *Vicitor*, Vol. 2, 1971, pp. 59–81.

1400 GLICK, Thomas F., 'New perspectives on the Hisba and its Hispanic derivatives', *Al-Qantara*, Vol. 8, No. 2, 1992, pp. 491–503.

1401 HABIB, Irfan, 'The system of bills of exchange (Hundis) in the Mughal empire', Muzaffarpur Session, *Proceedings of Indian History Congress*, 1972.

1402 HAILANI MUJI, Tahir, 'Islamic budgetary policy in theory and practice', Ph.D. dissertation, Abstract in *The American Journal of Islamic Social Sciences*, Vol. 9, No. 1, 1991, pp. 140–1.

1403 HAMOURI, Qasem, 'Rationality, time and accounting for the future in Islamic thought', in F.R. Faridi (ed.), *Essays in Islamic Economic Analysis*, New Delhi: Genuine Publications and Media, 1991, pp. 67–81.

1404 HAYASHI, Toshikazu, *On Islamic Accounting: Its Future Impact on Western Accounting*, Working Paper Series No. 18, Tokyo: Institute of Middle Eastern Studies, 1989.

1405 No entry.

1406 IQBAL, Zubair, *Public Finance in Islam*, Lahore: Readers Publishers, 1990, 126 pp.

1407 KAHF, Monzer, 'Fiscal and monetary policies in an Islamic economy', in Mohammad Ariff (ed.), *Monetary and Fiscal Economics of Islam*, Jeddah: International Centre for Research in Islamic Economics, King Abdul Aziz University, 1982, pp. 125–37.

1408 KHAN, Abdul Majid, 'Fiscal policy of an Islamic state', *The Universal Message*, Vol. 8, No. 6–7, 1986, pp. 32–5.

1409 KHAN, Muhammad Akram, 'Capital expenditure analysis in an Islamic framework', in S.G.S. Abod *et al.* (eds.), *An Introduction to Islamic Finance*, Kuala Lumpur: Quill Publishers, 1992, pp. 144–57.

1410 KHAN, Muhammad Akram, 'Role of the auditor in an Islamic economy', *Journal of Research in Islamic Economics* (Jeddah), Vol. 3, No. 1, 1985, pp. 31–44.

1411 KHAN, M. Fahim and KAHF, Monzer, 'Financing budget deficits through an Islamic secondary financial market', *New Horizon* (London), No. 393, June 1992, pp. 23–4.

1412 LAMBTON, A.K.S., 'Mongol fiscal administration in Persia', *Studia Islamica*, No. 64, 1986, pp. 79–100.

1413 MAYER, Ann Elizabeth, 'Islamization and taxation in Pakistan', in Anita M. Weiss (ed.), *Islamic Reassertion in Pakistan*, Lahore: Vanguard, 1987, pp. 59–78.

1414 MUKHERJI, Badal, 'A macro-model for the Islamic tax system', *Indian Economic Review*, Vol. 115, No. 1, 1980, pp. 65–75.

1415 NISSAR, Uddin, 'Fiscal policy in an Islamic state', in *Thoughts on Islamic Economics*, Dhaka: Islamic Economics Research Bureau, 1980, pp. 150–1.

1416 PEERZADE, Sayed Afzal, 'The genesis of supply-side tax policy in the Islamic system of taxation', Paper presented at the First All-India Conference on Islamic Economics, Bangalore, India, 27–28 June 1993.

1417 ROSE, Richard B., 'The Ottoman fiscal calendar', *Middle East Studies Association Bulletin* (Tucson, AZ), Vol. 25, No. 2, 1991, pp. 157–67.

1418 AL-SA'ADI, A.J.S., *Fiscal Policy in the Islamic State*, Newcastle-under-Lyme: Lyme Books, 1986, 272 pp.

1419 SALEEM, Shehzad, 'Zakat and tax system in Islam', *Renaissance* (Lahore), Vol. 2, No. 10, 1992, pp. 3–12.

1420 SATO, Tugitaka, 'Iqta policy of Sultan Baybars I', *Orient: Report of the Society for Near Eastern Studies in Japan*, Vol. 22, 1986, pp. 85–104.

1421 SIDDIQI, Muhammad Nejatullah, 'Public expenditure in an Islamic state', *Journal of Islamic Banking and Finance*, Vol. 4, No. 4, 1987, pp. 7–34.

1422 SIDDIQI, Muhammad Nejatullah, 'Public expenditure in an Islamic economy', in A.H.M. Sadeq *et al.* (eds.), *Development and Finance in Islam*, Selangor: International Islamic University Press, 1991, pp. 73–100.

1423 SIDDIQI, S.A., *Public Finance in Islam*, Lahore: Ashraf, 1975.

1424 SIDDIQI, Z., 'The Muhtesire under Aurangzeb', *Medieval India Quarterly*, 1963.

1425 SIDDIQUI, Azhar Hasan, 'The role of revenue collectors in Islam', Parts 1 and 2, *The Minaret International* (Karachi), Vol. 29, No. 2, 1992, pp. 11–20 and No. 3, 1992, pp. 21–8.

1426 SIDDIQUI, M. Yasin Mazhar, 'Role of booty in the economy during the Prophet's time', *Journal of Islamic Economics* (Jeddah), Vol. 1, 1989, pp. 83–116.

1427 SIMONSEN, J.B., *Studies in the Genesis and Early Development of the Caliphal Taxation System*, Copenhagen: Akademik Forlag, 1988.

1427a TABATABAI, Hossein Modarressi, *Kharaj in Islamic Law*, London: Brill, 1983.

1428 ZIADAH, N., *Al-Hisba and Al-Muhtasib in Islam*, Beirut: Catholic Press, 1962.

Institutions of Zakah

1429 ABU-BAKAR, Carmen A., 'Zakat and Sadaqa practices among the Moros of the Philippines', in M. Ariff (ed.), *The Islamic Voluntary Sector in Southeast Asia*, Pasir Panjang, Singapore: Institute of Southeast Asian Studies, 1991, pp. 168–91.

1430 ABU-SAUD, Mahmoud, *Contemporary Zakat*, Cincinnati, OH: Zakat Research Foundation, 1988, 199 pp.

1431 ALI, Shamsher, 'Structure and functions of Sadaqah and Zakah in Islam', *The Australian Minaret* (New South Wales), Vol. 3, 1988, pp. 27–30.

1432 ALLAM, Khaled Fouad, 'Solidarity in the Medina: past and present' (Zakah discussed), *Cooperazione* (Rome), June 1992, pp. 52–3.

1433 ANSARI, Abdul Rehman, *Zakah – The Religious Tax of Islam*, Bombay: Islamic Research Foundation, 1991, 32 pp.

1434 ARIFF, Muhammad, 'The Third International Zakah Conference' (Kuala Lumpur, Malaysia, 14–17 May 1990), *The American Journal of Islamic Social Sciences* (Herndon, VA), Vol. 7, No. 2, 1990, pp. 279–82.

1435 Association of Muslim Social Scientists of the US and Canada, *Some Aspects of Zakat: Proceedings of the Conference on Economics of Zakat* (13–14 April 1979), Plainfield, IN: American Trust Publications, 1980.

1436 KAMAL, Abdul Aziz, 'Zakat' (The prescribed charity), *Al-Islami* (Nairobi), Vol. 15, No. 1, 1991, pp. 16–20.

1437 KHOSA, Iqbal Ahmad, 'The institutions of Zakat', *Journal of Rural Development and Administration* (Peshawar), Vol. 21, No. 3, 1989, pp. 95–8.

1438 NADVI, S.H. Haq, 'Etymology of Zakat: the religious linguistic significance', *Arabic Studies* (Durban), Vol. 10, December 1986, pp. 101–8.

1439 'Report on the Third International Conference on Islamic Economics' (Kuala Lumpur, Malaysia, 28–30 January 1991), *Review of Islamic Economics* (Leicester), Vol. 2, No. 1, 1992, pp. 52–4.

1440 SATO, H., *Understanding Zakat: An Inquiry into the Methodological Problems of the Science of Economics*, Niigata: Institute of Middle Eastern Studies, 1987.

1441 SIDDIQI, Mohammad Akhtar Saeed, *Early Development of Zakat and Ijtihad*, Karachi: Islamic Research Academy, 1983.

Economic Role of Zakah

1442 AL-ABBADI, Abdul Salam, *Role of Zakat Funds in Contributing to Finance Development Projects*, Seminar paper, Niamey: Organization of the Islamic Conference, 1992.

1443 ABU WAHID, N.M., 'The economic implication of Zakah', *Contemporary Review*, Vol. 248, No. 1440, 1986, pp. 10–14.

1444 AHMAD, Afazuddin, 'Economic significance of Zakat', *Islamic Literature* (Lahore), August 1952, p. 5.

1445 AHMAD, Syed Thanvir, 'Economic significance of Zakat needs recognition', *Islamic Voice* (Bangalore), March 1993, p. 20.

1446 ANWAR, M., 'Channelling Zakah funds into long-term investments', *New Horizon* (London), No. 395, August–September 1992, pp. 18–20.

1447 ANWAR, M., Comment on 'Prospects of poverty eradication through the existing Zakat system in Pakistan' by Faiz Mohammad, *Pakistan Development Review*, Vol. 30, No. 4, 1991, pp. 1128–9.

1148 CLARK, Grace, 'Pakistan's Zakat and Ushr as a welfare system', in Anita M. Weiss (ed.), *Islamic Reassertion in Pakistan*, Lahore: Vanguard, 1987, pp. 79–96.

1449 EL-DIN, S.I. Tag, 'Allocative and stabilizing functions of Zakat in an Islamic economy', *Journal of Islamic Banking and Finance*, Vol. 3, No. 4, 1986, pp. 43–8.

1450 No entry.

1451 HASSAN, Nik Mustapha H., 'Zakat in Malaysia: present and future status', in A.H.M. Sadeq *et al.* (eds.), *Development and Finance in Islam*, Selangor: International Islamic University Press, 1991, pp. 213–38.

1452 ISLAM, M. Zohurul, 'Abstract of the socio-economic analysis of Al-Zakah', *Thoughts on Economics* (Dhaka), Vol. 7, No. 3, 1986, pp. 55–6.

1453 ISLAM, M. Zohurul *et al.*, *Zakah and Ushr: Socio-Economic Administrative Implications*, Research Monograph Series No. 2, Dhaka: Islamic Economics Research Bureau, 1988, 42 pp.

1454 'Is Zakat income tax?', *The Muslim Reader* (Singapore), Vol. 8, No. 4, 1989, pp. 6–7.

1455 MALIK, Shahnawaz, 'Lump-sum income transfer as a measure for rural poverty alleviation: Zakat and Ushr in Pakistan', *Journal of Rural Development and Administration* (Peshawar), Vol. 24, No. 2, 1992, pp. 98–101.

1456 MANNAN, Muhammad Abdul, 'Effects of Zakah assessment and collection on the redistribution of income in contemporary Muslim countries', in I.A. Imtiazi *et al.* (eds.), *Management of Zakah in Modern Muslim Society*, Jeddah: Islamic Research and Training Institute, Islamic Development Bank, 1989, pp. 29–50.

1457 MOHAMMAD, Faiz, 'Prospects of poverty eradication through the existing Zakat system in Pakistan', *Pakistan Development Review* (Islamabad), Vol. 30, No. 4, 1991, pp. 1119–25.

1458 RAHMAN, Abdel Moussa Ibrahim, 'Zakah, Social Justice and Social Security', in *Outlines of Islamic Economics*, Indianapolis: Association of Muslim Social Scientists, 1977.

1459 SHEHATAH, S. Ismail, 'Limitations on the use of Zakah funds in financing the socio-economic infrastructure of society', in I.A. Imtiazi *et al.* (eds.), *Management of Zakah in Modern Muslim Society*, Jeddah: Islamic Research and Training Institute, Islamic Development Bank, 1989, pp. 57–73.

1460 *Survey of Social and Economic Impact of Zakat and Ushr on Individuals and Households*, Karachi: Statistics Division, Federal Bureau of Statistics, Government of Pakistan, 1988, 129 pp.

1461 ZAIM, Sabahaddin, 'Recent interpretations of the economic aspects of Zakah', in I.A. Imtiazi *et al.* (eds.), *Management of Zakah in Modern Muslim Society*, Jeddah: Islamic Research and Training Institute, Islamic Development Bank, 1989, pp. 101–20.

Administration of Zakah

1462 ABDULLAH, Taufik, 'Zakat collection and distribution in Indonesia', in M. Ariff (ed.), *The Islamic Voluntary Sector in Southeast*

Asia, Pasir Panjang, Singapore: Institute of Southeast Asian Studies, 1991, pp. 50–84.

1463 GHAZALI, Aidit Bin, 'Zakat administration in Malaysia', in M. Ariff (ed.), *The Islamic Voluntary Sector in Southeast Asia*, Pasir Panjang, Singapore: Institute of Southeast Asian Studies, 1991, pp. 85–117.

1464 IMTIAZI, I.A., 'Organization of Zakah. The Pakistan model and experience', in I.A. Imtiazi *et al.* (eds.), *Management of Zakah in Modern Muslim Society*, Jeddah: Islamic Research and Training Institute, Islamic Development Bank, 1989, pp. 157–76.

1465 IMTIAZI, I.A. *et al.* (eds.), *Management of Zakah in Modern Muslim Society*, Jeddah: Islamic Research and Training Institute, Islamic Development Bank, 1989, 236 pp.

1466 KAHF, Monzer, *Zakah Management in Some Muslim Societies*, Jeddah: Islamic Research and Training Institute, Islamic Development Bank, 1993, 54 pp.

1467 KHAN, Muhammad Akram, *Organising Zakah: A Model of Legal Administrative and Financial Control*, Lahore: All-Pakistan Islamic Education Congress, 1990, 38 pp.

1468 KISTER, M.J., 'The social and political implications of three traditions in the Kitab al-Kharaj of Yahya b. Adam', *Journal of the Economic and Social History of the Orient* (Leiden), Vol. 3, Part 1, 1960, pp. 326–34.

1469 AL-OMAR, Fuad A., 'Management of Zakah through semi-government institutions', in I.A. Imtiazi *et al.* (eds.), *Management of Zakah in Modern Muslim Society*, Jeddah: Islamic Research and Training Institute, Islamic Development Bank, 1989, pp. 131–52.

1470 AL-ZEHILY, Mohammad, 'The ways of distributing alms – Zakat', *Risalat al-Jihad* (Paola, Malta), No. 74, Autumn 1990, pp. 153–6.

Law on Zakah

1471 CALDER, N., 'Zakat in Imami Shi jurisprudence, from the 10th to the 16th century AD', *Bulletin of the School of Oriental and African Studies* (London), Vol. 44, No. 3, 1981, pp. 468–80.

1472 KAHF, Monzer, 'Zakat: unresolved issues in the contemporary Fiqh', *Journal of Islamic Economics* (Kuala Lumpur), Vol. 2, No. 1, 1989, pp. 1–22.

1473 MAGHNIYYAH, Allama Muhammad Jawad, 'Zakah and Khums, according to fifth school of Islamic law', *Al-Tawhid* (Tehran), Vol. 10, No. 1, 1992, pp. 123–38.

1474 SIDDIQI, M.A. Sayeed, *Early Development of Zakat Law and Ijtihad*, Karachi: Islamic Research Academy, 1983, 248 pp.

1475 ZAYAS, Farishta G. De, *Law and Philosophy of Zakat: The Islamic Welfare System*, Damascus: Al-Jadidah, 1960, 420 pp.

Other Sources of Revenue

1476 AHMAD, Q., 'The comparative analysis of agricultural income tax with another: a case study of Nawbash', *Pakistan Economic and Social Review*, Vol. 28, No. 2, 1988, pp. 109–26.

1477 AKHTAR, Syed Mahamood, 'Jiziyah: capitation tax in an Islamic state', Parts 1 and 2, *Yaqeen International* (Karachi), Vol. 38, No. 5, 1989, pp. 53–4, 55 and No. 6, 1989, pp. 65–7.

1478 ATHAMINA, Khalil, 'Taxation reforms in early Islamic Khurasan: a reassessment', *Der Islam*, Vol. 65, No. 4, 1988, pp. 272–81.

1479 BAILLIE, Neil B.E., 'Of the Kharaj or Muhammadan land tax, its application to British India, and effect on the tenure of land', *Journal of the Royal Asiatic Society* (Bombay), No. 7, 1875, pp. 172–88.

1480 BEN-SHEMESH, A., *Taxation in Islam*, Vol. 2, *Quddama B. Jafar's Kitab al-Kharaj, Part 7, and Excerpts from Abu-Yusuf's Kitab al-Kharaj*, Leiden: Brill and London: Luzac, 1965.

1481 CASTORINA, Camille P., Review article on *Islamic Taxation in the Classic Period with Special Reference to Circumstances in Iraq* by F. Lokkegaard, in *Journal of Economic Literature*, Vol. 13, March 1980, pp. 131–2.

1482 CHANDRA, S., 'Jiziyah and the state in India during the seventeenth century', *Journal of the Economic and Social History of the Orient* (Leiden), Vol. 12, 1969.

1483 EL-FADL, Khaled Abou, 'Tax farming in Islamic law (Qibalah and Daman of Kharaj): a search for concept', *Islamic Studies* (Islamabad), Vol. 31, No. 1, 1992, pp. 5–32.

1484 GOITEIN, S.D., 'Evidence on the Muslim poll tax from non-Muslim sources. A Geniza study', *Journal of the Economic and Social History of the Orient*, Vol. 6, 1963, pp. 278–95.

1485 No entry.

1486 LOKKEGAARD, F., *Islamic Taxation in the Classical Period*, Copenhagen: Branner of Korch, 1950, 280 pp. Also Lahore: Suid Sagar Academy, 1979, 286 pp.

1487 MAYER, Ann Elizabeth, 'Islamization and taxation in Pakistan', in Anita M. Wein (ed.), *Islamic Reassertion in Pakistan*, Lahore: Vanguard, 1987, pp. 59–78.

1488 MEERA, A.K.M. and AHSAN, S.N., 'Al-Khraj and related issues: a comparative study of early Islamic scholarly thought and their receptiveness by Western economists', in A.H.M. Sadeq and A. Ghazali (eds.), *Readings in Islamic Economic Thought*, Petaling Jaya: Longman Malaysia, 1992, pp. 203–21.

1489 MULLA, Jiwan, *Muhammadan Law on Tax*, tr. from the *Futawa Alamgiri* with explanatory notes and an introductory essay by Neil B.E. Baillie, Lahore: Aziz Publishers, 1979, 134 pp.

1490 OSMAN, Muhammad Fathi M., *Juristic Rules of Conquered Land and Taxation: Fay and Khamis: Their Origin and Development in Medieval Islam*, Princeton, NJ: Princeton University Press, 1976, 634 pp.

1491 SACHEDINA, Abdulaziz, 'Al-Khums: the fifth in the Imami Shi'i legal system', *Journal of Near Eastern Studies* (Chicago), Vol. 39, 1980, pp. 275–89.

1492 SHAD, Abdul Rahman, *Zakat and Ushr*, Lahore: Kazi Publications, 1986.

1493 TABATABAI, Hossein Modarressi, 'Kharaj in Shia law from the beginning to the 10th/16th century', Ph.D. dissertation, University of Oxford, 1982, 439 pp.

1494 TABATABAI, Hossein Modarressi, *Kharaj in Islamic Law*, London: Brill, 1983, 203 pp.

Waqf

1495 ABDALLAHI, A.A., 'A new definition of Waqf: on the basis of which the legal personality of Waqf is established', *Journal of Islamic and Comparative Law* (London), Vol. 7 (bis), 1978, pp. 57–72.

1496 AHMAD, Ziauddin, 'Waqf as an instrument of perpetuity – an assessment', *Islamic Studies*, Vol. 26, No. 2, 1987, pp. 127–42.

1497 ALHABSHI, Syed Othman, 'Waqf management in Malaysia', in M. Ariff (ed.), *The Islamic Voluntary Sector in Southeast Asia*, Pasir Panjang, Singapore: Institute of Southeast Asian Studies, 1991, pp. 118–37.

1498 No entry.

1499 ANDERSON, J.N.D., 'Waqf in East Africa', *The Journal of African Law*, Vol. 3, 1959, pp. 152–64.

1500 BAER, Gabriel, 'Jerusalem's families of notables and the Waqf in the early nineteenth century', in David Kushner (ed.), *Palestine in the Late Ottoman Period*, Leiden, Brill, 1986, pp. 109–22.

1501 BAER, Gabriel, 'Waqf reform in Egypt', *St Antony's Papers* (Oxford), Vol. 4, 1958, pp. 61–76.

1502 BASAR, Hasmat (ed.), *Management and Development of Waqf Properties*, Jeddah: Islamic Research and Training Institute, Islamic Development Bank, 1987, 161 pp.

1503 'Charities (Waqfs) in Turkish life' (Past and present), *Turkish Review Quarterly Digest* (Ankara), Vol. 3, No. 17, 1989, pp. 71–81.

1504 DEGUILHEM SCHOEM, Randi, 'The loan of Mursad on Waqf properties', in Farhad Kazemi and R.D. McChesney (eds.), *A Way Prepared: Essays on Islamic Culture in Honor of Richard Bayley Winder*, New York: New York University Press, 1988, pp. 68–79.

1505 FAROOQI, Muhammad Yousuf, 'The institution of Waqf in historical perspective' (India), *Hamdard Islamicus* (Karachi), Vol. 13, No. 1, 1990, pp. 25–31.

1506 HUSAIN, Aftab S., 'Classification and condition of Awqaf', *Hamdard Islamicus* (Karachi), Vol. 12, No. 3, 1989, pp. 3–28.

1507 'India: the Waqf Act 1954 – as amended by Waqf (Amendment) Act of 1984', *Islamic and Comparative Law Quarterly* (New Delhi), Vol. 5, No. 1, 1985, pp. 4–80.

1508 ISLAM, Zafarul, Review article on *Waqf in India: A Study of Administrative and Statutory Control*, in *Journal of Objective Studies* (Aligarh), Vol. 3, No. 1, 1991, pp. 195–201.

1509 KHAN, Ateeq, 'Waqf administration in UP – a legislative retrospect', *Islam and the Modern Age* (New Delhi), Vol. 21, No. 1, 1990, pp. 53–75.

1510 KHAN, Ateeque, 'India: the Waqf (Amendment) Act 1984 – a plea for reconsideration', *Islamic and Comparative Law Quarterly* (New Delhi), Vol. 5, No. 1, 1985, pp. 85–90.

1511 KHAN, Imtiaz Ahmad, *What is Waqf?*, Delhi: Idarah-i-Adabiyat-i-Delli, 1988, 92 pp.

1512 MANDAVILLE, J.E., 'Usurious piety: the cash Waqf controversy in the Ottoman empire', *International Journal of Middle East Studies*, Vol. 10, No. 3, 1979, pp. 289–308.

1513 MCCHESNEY, R.D., *Waqf in Central Asia: Four Hundred Years in the History of a Muslim Shrine, 1480–1889*, Princeton, NJ: Princeton University Press, 1991.

1514 MCCHESNEY, R.D., 'Waqf in Balakh and Bukhara in the second half of the 11th–17th century', *Hamdard Islamicus* (Karachi), Vol. 12, No. 2, 1989, pp. 39–56.

1515 ODED, Peri, 'Waqf and Ottoman welfare policy: the poor kitchen of Hasseki Sultan in eighteenth-century Jerusalem', *Journal of the Economic and Social History of the Orient* (Leiden), Vol. 25, No. 2, 1992, pp. 167–86.

1516 OTHMAN, Mohammad Zain bin Haji, 'Institution of Waqf', *Islamic Culture* (Hyderabad), Vol. 58, 1984, pp. 55–62.

1517 OTHMAN, Mohammad Zain bin Haji, 'Origin of the institution of Waqf', *Hamdard Islamicus* (Karachi), Vol. 6, No. 2, 1983, pp. 3–23.

1518 PATHUSHA, K.M., 'Problems of Awkaf and Mutalawallis in Tamil Nadu' (India), *Journal of Objective Studies* (Aligarh), Vol. 4, No. 1, July 1992, pp. 136–41.

1519 PRAERTCHOB, Preeda, 'Mobilization of resources through Waqf in Thailand', in M. Ariff (ed.), *The Islamic Voluntary Sector in Southeast Asia*, Pasir Panjang, Singapore: Institute of Southeast Asian Studies, 1991, pp. 233–58.

1520 RABIE, Hassanein, 'Some financial aspects of the Waqf system in medieval Egypt', *Egyptian Historical Review*, Vol. 18, 1971, pp. 1–24.

1521 RASHID, Syed Khalid, *Waqf Administration in India: Socio-Legal Study*, New Delhi: Vikas, 1978, 189 pp.

1522 RASHID, Syed Khalid, 'How to streamline Awkaf in India', *Radiance Views Weekly* (New Delhi), Vol. 27, No. 24, 1992, pp. 75–7.

1523 REILLY, James, 'Rural Waqfs of Ottoman Damascus, rights of ownership, possession and tenancy', *Acta Orientalia* (Copenhagen), Vol. 51, 1990, pp. 27–47.

1524 RODED, Ruth, 'Quantitative analysis of Waqf endowment deeds: a pilot project' (Ottoman Turkey), *The Journal of Ottoman Studies* (Istanbul), Vol. 9, 1989, pp. 51–76.

1525 No entry.

1526 SAARISALO, A., 'The Turkish Waqf', *Studia Orientalia*, Vol. 19, No. 10, 1953, p. 6.

1527 SUHRAWARDY, A. Al-Ma'mun, 'The Waqf of moveables', *Journal and Proceedings of the Asiatic Society of Bengal*, No. 7, 1911, pp. 323–430.

1528 TAWFIQ, Muhammad Amin, 'Development of Awqaf system in Egypt', *Majallat al-Azhar* (Cairo), Vol. 47, No. 6, 1975, pp. 11–16.

1529 *Waqf in India: A Study of Administrative and Statutory Control*, New Delhi: Gian Publishing House, 1990.

1530 WILLIAMS, John Alden, 'Waqf', in *The Encyclopaedia of Religion*, Vol. 15, London: Macmillan, 1987, pp. 337–9.

Waqf under Islamic Law

1531 AL-AMIN, Hassan Abdullah, 'Waqf in Islamic jurisprudence', in Hasmet Basar (ed.), *Management and Development of Awqaf Properties*, Jeddah, Islamic Research and Training Institute, Islamic Development Bank, 1987, pp. 15–18.

1532 BEG, M.H., 'Gifts, family Waqfs and pre-emption under Islamic law: some observations', in Tahir Mahmood (ed.), *Islamic Law in Modern India*, Bombay, 1972, pp. 209–12.

1533 CATTAN, H., 'The law of Waqf', *Law in the Middle East*, 1955, pp. 203–22.

1534 CRECELIUS, Daniel, 'Incidences of Waqf cases in three Cairo courts, 1640–1802', *Journal of the Economic and Social History of the Orient* (Leiden), Vol. 29, No. 2, 1986, pp. 176–89.

1535 GOADBY, F.M., 'Law and jurisdiction in Palestine in matters of personal status and Waqf', *L'Egypte Contemporaine*, Vol. 17, 1926, pp. 127–49.

1536 GOADBY, F.M., 'Muslim law in the Egyptian mixed courts – Wakf', *Journal of Comparative Legislation and International Law*, Vol. 10, 1928, pp. 317–19; Vol. 11, 1929, pp. 278–9; Vol. 16, 1934, pp. 40–52.

1537 GOADBY, F.M., 'Waqf in Egypt', *Journal of Comparative Legislation and International Law*, Vol. 10, 1928, pp. 319–20.

1538 HAQ, M. Nurual, 'Development of the law of Wakf through legislation in Bangladesh', *Law and International Affairs* (Dhaka), Vol. 11, 1986, pp. 103–11.

1539 LAYISH, Aharon, 'The Maliki family Waqf, according to will and Waqfiyyat', *Bulletin of the School of Oriental and African Studies* (London), Vol. 46, 1983, pp. 1–32.

1540 LAYISH, Aharon, 'The Muslim Waqf in Israel', *Asian and African Studies*, Vol 2, 1966, pp. 71–6.

1541 MAGHNIYYAH, Allama Muhammad Jawad, 'Waqf, according to fifth school of Islamic law', *Al-Tawhid* (Tehran), Vol. 8, No. 1, 1990, pp. 61–8.

1542 MAHMOOD, Tahir, 'Islamic family Waqf in twentieth-century legislation: a comparative perspective', *Islamic and Comparative Law Quarterly* (New Delhi), Vol. 8, No. 1, 1988, pp. 1–20.

1543 NAQVI, Syed H.M. and MAHMUDDIN, Nasir Syed, *Law of Waqfs: Being a Full Commentary with Complete Case Law and the West Pakistan Wakf Properties Ordinance (XXVII of 1961) with East Pakistan Wakf Ordinance, 1962*, Lahore, 1968, 159 + 33 pp.

1544 RASHID, Syed Khalid, *Waqf Laws and Administration in India*, Lucknow: 1973, 184 pp.

1545 SCHACHT, J., 'Early doctrines on Waqf', *Mélanges Köprülü*, 1953, pp. 443–52.

1546 YUSOOF, M. Mohammad, *Review of the Mohammadan Law of the Wakf*, Calcutta, 1906.

1547 ZAID, Abdul Aziz Muhammad, *The Islamic Law of Bequest*, London: Scorpion, 1986, 296 pp.

16

ISLAMIC COMMERCIAL LAWS

General

1548 ABUMOUAMER, Faris Mahmoud, 'An analysis of the role and function of the Sharia control in Islamic banks', Ph.D. dissertation, University College Cardiff (Wales), 1989, 561 pp.

1549 AGHNIDES, Nicolas P., *Mohammedan Theories of Finance with an Introduction to Mohammedan Law and a Bibliography*, New York: AMS Press, 1969.

1550 AHMAD, Khurshid, Review article on *Unlawful Gain and Legitimate Profit in Islamic Law: Riba, Gharar and Islamic Banking* by Nabil A. Saleh, in *The Muslim World Book Review* (Leicester), Vol. 9, No. 3, 1989, pp. 24–30.

1551 AKHTAR, A.R., *The Law and Practice of Interest-Free Banking, with Banking Tribunals Ordinance (Pakistan)*, Lahore: Mansoor Book House, 1988, 200 pp.

1552 AMIN, S.H., 'Arbitration law in Iran: postrevolutionary changes – Part 1, International Commercial Arbitration', *Middle East Executive Reports*, Vol. 11, No. 8, 1988, pp. 10, 14–16.

1553 AMIN, S.H., *Commercial Arbitration in Islamic and Iranian Law*, Tehran: Vahid Publications, 1990, 504 pp.

1554 AMIN, S.H., *Islamic Law and Its Implications for the Modern World* (Including an essay on Islamic banking), Glasgow: Royston Ltd, 1989, 399 pp.

1555 'The Amman Arab Convention on Commercial Arbitration', *Arab Law Quarterly* (London), Vol. 7, No. 1, 1992, pp. 83–92.

1556 ANDERSON, J.N.D., 'Islamic law of testate and intestate succession and the administration of deceased persons' assets', in Tahir Mahmood (ed.), *Islamic Law in Modern India*, Bombay, 1972, pp. 202–6.

1557 ANDERSON, J.N.D., 'Recent reforms in the Islamic law of inheritance', *International and Comparative Law Quarterly*, Vol. 14, 1965, pp. 349–65.

1558 ARIFF, Mohammad, 'Towards the Shri'ah paradigm of Islamic economics: the beginning of a scientific revolution', *American Journal of Islamic Social Sciences*, 1979, Vol. 2, No. 1.

1559 ARTHOUR, Gloor (ed.), *Islamic Law and Business*, Zurich: Arab–Swiss Chamber of Commerce and Industry, 1982.

1559a AVANESSIAN, Aida, 'The new legal system – Iran', *Middle East Economic Digest*, 1 March 1991, p. 17.

1560 BADAWI, Zaki, 'Islamic law and international commercial disputes', *Banking and Trade*, No. 1, Spring 1987, pp. 18–19.

1561 AL-BARRAK, A.R., *Application of Islamic Law to Taxation in Saudi Arabia*, Exeter: University of Exeter, 1981, 218 pp.

1562 BAUBEN, Jabal M., 'A comparative study of the Islamic law of inheritance and Fante customary law of inheritance', *Bulletin on Islam and Christian–Muslim Relations in Africa*, Vol. 4, No. 4, 1986, pp. 1–26.

1563 CANNON, Bycon, *Politics of Law and the Courts in Nineteenth-Century Egypt*, Salt Lake City, UT: University of Utah Press, 1988.

1564 COULSON, Noel J., *Commercial Law in the Gulf States: The Islamic Legal Tradition*, London: Graham and Trotman, 1984, 108 pp.

1565 DARRAT, Ali F., 'Are checking accounts in American banks permissible under Islamic laws? A note', *The American Journal of Islamic Social Sciences* (Herndon, VA), Vol. 2, No. 1, 1985, pp. 101–3.

1566 EDGE, Jan, 'Comparative commercial law of Egypt and the Arabian Gulf', *Cleveland State Law Review*, No. 34, 1985–6, pp. 129–44.

1567 GAIANI, A., 'The juridical nature of the modern Qirad', *East and West* (Rome), 1953, pp. 81–6.

1568 GAMAL, M. Badr, BASSIOUNI, M.S. and DORPH, Ken, *Interest and Banking in Islamic Law*, Chicago: Mid-America Chamber of Commerce, 1990, 59 pp.

1569 GERALD, J., 'Legal aspects of doing business in Kuwait', *Arab Law Quarterly*, Vol. 6, No. 4, 1991, pp. 322–30.

1570 GERBER, Haim, 'The Muslim law of partnership in Ottoman court records', *Studia Islamica*, Vol. 53, 1981, pp. 109–19.

1571 GHAMIDI, Javed Ahmad, 'The Islamic law of inheritance', Parts 1 and 2, Tr. S. Saleem, *Renaissance* (Lahore), Vol. 1, No. 9, 1991, pp. 11–21 and No. 10, 1991, pp. 7–17.

1572 No entry.

1573 HASSAN, Hussein Hamid, 'Financial intermediation in the framework of Shri'ah', in M. Ariff and M.A. Mannan (eds.), *Developing a System of Financial Instruments*, Jeddah: Islamic Development Bank, 1990, pp. 27–48.

1574 HASSAN, Hussein Hamid, 'The jurisprudence of financial transactions' (Fiqh al-Mu'amalat), in A. Ahmad and K.R. Awan (eds.), *Lectures on Islamic Economics*, Jeddah: Islamic Development Bank, 1992, pp. 105–15.

1575 HOMOOD, S.H., *Islamic Banking: The Adaptation of Banking Practice to Conform with Islamic Law*, Pittsburgh, PA: University of Pittsburgh Press, 1984, 283 pp.

1576 No entry.

1577 'Islamic banking and the law', *New Horizon*, No. 390, 1992, p. 2.

1578 JOHANSEN, Baber, *The Islamic Law on Land Tax and Rent*, London: Croom Helm, 1937, 176 pp.

1579 KARAM, N.H. (ed.), *Business Laws of the United Arab Emirates*, London: Graham and Trotman, 1990, 1200 pp.

1580 KARAM, N.H. (ed.), *Business Laws of Kuwait*, London: Graham and Trotman, 1990, 1000 pp.

1581 KARAM, N.H. (ed.), *Business Laws of Iraq*, London: Graham and Trotman, 1990, 1000 pp.

1582 KARAM, N.H. (ed.), *Business Laws of Egypt*, London: Graham and Trotman, 1990, 800 pp.

1583 KHADDURI, Majid, 'Equity and Islamic law', in George N. Atiyeh and Ibrahim W. Oweiss (eds.), *Arab Civilization, Challenges and Responses*, New York: State University of New York Press, 1988, pp. 82–7.

1584 KHAN, Muhammad Akram, Review of *Islamic Banking: The Adaptation of Banking Practice to Conform with Islamic Law* by S.H. Homood, in *The Muslim World Book Review*, Vol. 7, No. 2, 1987, pp. 51–3.

1585 No entry.

1586 MACKEEN, Abdul Majid, 'Islamic fiscal and property laws in Malaysia', in M.B. Hooker (ed.), *Malaysian Legal Essays*, Malaysia. Malayan Law Journal, 1986, pp. 263–90.

1587 MALLAT, Chibli (ed.), *Islamic Law and Finance*, London: School of Oriental and African Studies, 1988, 140 pp.

1588 MAYER, A.E., 'Islamic law and banking in the Middle East today', *Middle East Executive Report*, 1979.

1589 MUSLEHUDDIN, M., *Banking and Islamic Law*, Karachi: Islamic Research Academy, 1974, 153 pp.

1590 MUSLEHUDDIN, M., *Insurance and Islamic Law*, Lahore, 1969, 202 pp.

1591 MUTAWAKIL, G., *Business and Law in Saudi Arabia*, Falcon Press, n.d., 219 pp.

1591a OMER, A.I., 'Grandfather *vis-à-vis* collaterals in the Islamic law of inheritance', *Islamic Studies*, Vol. 28, No. 4, 1989, pp. 363–76.

1592 PARKER, Mushtak, 'Arbitration: keeping the wheels of trade turning', *The Middle East* (London), August 1987, pp. 27–8.

1593 POWERS, D.S., *Studies in Qur'an and Hadith: The Formation of the Islamic Law of Inheritance*, Berkeley and Los Angeles: University of California Press, 1986, 264 pp.

1594 RAGIE, Zahier Ahmad, 'Some ethical principles of business as explained in the Sunnah', *Al-Balagh* (Karachi), Vol. 1, No. 9, 1991, pp. 13–16.

1595 RAHNEMA, Ali and NOMANI, Fouad, *Islamic Economic System*, London: Zed, 1992, 192 pp.

1596 SALEH, Nabil A., *Unlawful Gain and Legitimate Profit in Islamic Law: Riba, Gharar and Islamic Banking*, Cambridge: Cambridge University Press, 1986, 130 pp.

1597 SALEL, Samir, *Commercial Arbitration in the Arab Middle East: A Study in Shari'ah and Statute Law*, Lahore, 1984.

1598 EL SARRAF, M. Fouad, 'Money market dealings within the framework of the Islamic law', *Journal of Islamic Banking and Finance* (Karachi), Vol. 1, Spring 1984, pp. 57–64.

1599 EL SHARIF, Bagat Khalil, 'Law and practice of profit-sharing in Islamic banking with particular reference to Mudaraba and Murabaha', Ph.D. dissertation, University of Exeter, 1990, 374 pp.

1599a 'The law for usury (interest)-free banking', *Journal of Islamic Banking and Finance*, Vol. 3, No. 4, 1986, pp. 69–78.

1600 TOMKIN, Cyril and ABDUL KARIM, Rifat Ahmed, 'The Sharia'ah and its implications for Islamic financial analysis: an opportunity to study interactions among society, organization and accounting', *The American Journal of Islamic Social Sciences*, Vol. 4, No. 1, 1987, pp. 101–15.

1601 USMANI, Muhammad Taqi, 'The principle of limited liability from the Shari'ah viewpoint', *New Horizon* (London), No. 395, 1992, pp. 21–2.

1602 USMANI, Muhammad Taqi, 'The role of religious boards in developing interest-free economy', *Al-Balagh* (Karachi), Vol. 1, No. 3, 1990, pp. 19–22.

1602a ZAMAN, Hasanuz S.M., 'The liability of partners in the Islamic Shari'ah', *Islamic Studies* (Islamabad), Vol. 10, No. 4, December 1971, pp. 319–41.

1603 ZARQA, Mohammad Anas, 'Islamic jurisprudence (Fiqh) and economics of exchange', in A. Ahmad and K.R. Awan (eds.), *Lectures on Islamic Economics*, Jeddah: Islamic Development Bank, 1992, pp. 93–104.

Islamic Contract Law

1604 AMIN, S.H., *Remedies for Breach of Contract in Islamic and Iranian Law*, Glasgow: Royston Press, 1984, 264 pp.

1605 FRANTZ-MURPHY, Gladys, 'A comparison of Arabic and earlier Egyptian contract formularies, Part 5, Formulaic evidence', *Journal of Near Eastern Studies* (Chicago), Vol. 48, No. 2, 1989, pp. 97–109.

1606 HAMID, M.F., 'The freedom to make stipulations in the Islamic law of contract', *Journal of Islamic and Comparative Law* (London), Vol. 6, 1976, pp. 22–32.

1607 HAMID, M.F., *Role of Consent in Formation of Contracts: A Comparative Study in English and Islamic Law*, London: School of Oriental and African Studies, 1972.

1608 HAMID, M.F., 'Misrepresentation as a vice of consent in the Islamic law of contracts', *Sudan Law Journal and Reports*, 1972, pp. 84–102.

1609 HAMID, M.F., 'Mutual assent in the formation of contracts in Islamic Law', *Journal of Islamic and Comparative Law* (London), Vol. 7, 1977, pp. 41–53.

1610 HAMID, M.F., 'Does the Islamic law of contract recognize a doctrine of mistake?', *Journal of Islamic and Comparative Law* (London), Vol. 4, 1972, pp. 1–16.

1611 HAMID, M.F., 'Islamic law of contracts', *Journal of Islamic and Comparative Law* (London), Vol. 3, 1969, pp. 1–10.

1612 KHAN, Tariqullah, *Contractual International Investments: Relevance for Islamic Economics*, Jeddah: Islamic Research and Training Institute, Islamic Development Bank, 1991, 54 pp.

1613 KHOURIDES, Nicholas P., 'The influence of Islamic law on contemporary Middle Eastern legal system: the formulation and binding force of contracts', *Columbia Journal of Transnational Law*, Vol. 9, No. 2, 1970.

1614 MOHAMED, Abdalla I., 'Stipulations for the benefit of third parties in Islamic law of contracts', *Journal of Islamic and Comparative Law* (London), Vol. 9, 1980, pp. 7–20.

1615 MUSA, Muhammad Yusuf, 'The liberty of the individual in contracts and conditions according to Islamic law', *Islamic Quarterly* (London), Vol. 2, 1955, pp. 79–85, 252–63.

1616 NIAZI, Liaqat Ali Khan, *Islamic Law of Contract*, Lahore: Research Cell, Dayat Singh Trust Library, 1991, 511 pp.

1617 AR-RAWI, Abdul Jalil, 'Principle of the Islamic law of contracts', *George Washington Law Review*, 1953, pp. 32–9.

1618 RAYNER, Susan, *Theory of Contracts in Islamic Law: A Comparative Analysis With Particular Reference to Modern Legislation in Kuwait, Bahrain and the UAE*, London: Graham and Trotman, 1991, 450 pp.

1619 'Saudi Arabia: example of Ministry of Finance contract review', *Middle East Executive Report*, Vol. 7, No. 12, 1984, pp. 26–7.

1619a SAXENA, I.C., 'Justice Mahmood on contract law', Mahmood number, *Aligarh Law Journal*, Vol. 5, 1973, pp. 75–9.

1620 SHIMIZU, Hideyuki, *Philosophy of the Islamic Law of Contract: A Comparative Study of Contractual Justice*, IMES Working Paper Series No. 15, Niigata-ken: Institute of Middle Eastern Studies, 1989, 131 pp.

1621 'The new contract law in Sudan: civil transaction law of April 1984', *Arabia* (London), Vol. 4, No. 36, 1984, pp. 62–3.

Appendix

SERIAL PUBLICATIONS ON ISLAMIC ECONOMICS

The American Journal of Islamic Finance (1990–)
This journal is a review of the issues and business in the field of Islamic finance, and aims to promote the understanding of the subject. Also contains news on the functioning of Islamic banks as well as book reviews. For subscription information, contact: Abdul Kader, Publishers, *The American Journal of Islamic Finance*, 27957 Ridgebluff Court, Rancho Palos Verdes, CA 90274, USA.

The American Journal of Islamic Social Sciences (1984–; 4 times a year; ISSN 0742-6763)
Published by the International Institute of Islamic Thought, this journal deals with the new and exciting field of the Islamization of knowledge, the relevancy of Islamic economics to modern times. Also contains book reviews, research notes, seminar and conference reports, and abstracts of Ph.D. dissertations on Islamic economics and finance. For subscription information, contact: Subscription Department, *The American Journal of Islamic Social Sciences*, PO Box 669, Herndon, VA 22070, USA.

Islamic Economics News Bulletin (1991–; 6 times a year)
Published by the Indian Association for Islamic Economics, this news bulletin aims to create awareness of the latest developments in the theory and practice of Islamic economics. Also contains book reviews and research in progress. For subscription information, contact: Editor, *Islamic Economics News Bulletin*, 4-1212 Sir Syed Nagar, Aligarh 202002, India.

Islamic Economics Studies (1993–, twice a year)
Published by the Islamic Research and Training Institute of the Islamic Development Bank, this journal covers Islamic economics, finance and

banking. Contains articles, discussion papers, seminar/conference reports, annotated listings and book reviews. For subscription information, contact: Islamic Research and Training Institute, Islamic Development Bank, PO Box 9201, Jeddah, Saudi Arabia.

The Journal of Humanomics
This journal focuses on the intellectual enquiry into the theory and policy emanating from an endogenous treatment of ethics and values in economic knowledge. Also publishes full-length papers, book reviews and short papers in the field of ethico-economics. Some specific areas are: economic philosophy and challenge to mainstream economics; theory of justice, social games and strategies; critique of economic thought and economic historicism; welfare economics with ethical elements; and religious foundation of economic theory and policy. For subscription information, contact: Centre of Humanomics, Department of Social Sciences, University College of Cape Breton, Sydney, Nova Scotia, B1P 6L2, Canada.

Journal of Islamic Banking and Finance (1984–; 4 times a year)
Published by the International Association of Islamic Banks, this journal provides a forum for debate on Islamic economics and finance. Also contains book reviews. For subscription information, contact: Subscription Department, B-5 (1st Floor), Kahkashan Apartment, Block No. 7, Main Clinton Road, Karachi, Pakistan.

Journal of Islamic Economics (1988–; twice a year; ISSN 0128-0066)
Published in English, Malay and Arabic by the International Islamic University, this journal is devoted to facilitating communication and discussion on research in the field of economics, particularly business accounting in the sphere of Fiqh related to economics or business. For subscription information, contact: Editor-in-Chief, *Journal of Islamic Economics*, Kulliyyah of Economics and Management, International Islamic University, PO Box 70, Jalan Sultan, 46700 Petaling Jaya, Selangor, Malaysia.

Journal of King Abdul Aziz University: Islamic Economics (1989–; once a year)
Published in English and Arabic (separate sections) by the Centre of Research in Islamic Economics, King Abdul Aziz University, this journal is concerned with theoretical research in Islamic economics. Empirical studies that have important theoretical implications are

included within its scope, as are research papers containing critiques from the Islamic point of view of well-known economic hypotheses. There are also short notes, research in progress, a discussion forum, and reviews and abstracts. For subscription information, contact: Editor-in-Chief, *Journal of King Abdul Aziz University: Islamic Economics*, Centre for Research in Islamic Economics, King Abdul Aziz University, PO Box 16711, Jeddah, Saudi Arabia.

The Muslim World Book Review (1980–; 4 times a year; ISSN 0260 3063)
Published by the Islamic Foundation, Leicester, UK, and the International Institute of Islamic Thought, Herndon, Virginia, USA, this journal, accompanied by its supplement, *Index of Islamic Literature*, aims to present the Muslim viewpoint on books and issues which concern Islam and Muslims. The journal provides detailed critical reviews, brief introductions and select bibliographies on recent and contemporary publications on Islamic economics. For subscription information, contact: *The Muslim World Book Review*, The Islamic Foundation, Markfield Dawah Centre, Ratby Lane, Markfield, Leicester LE6 9RN, UK.

New Horizon (12 times a year)
Published as an official organ of the Institute of Islamic Banking and Finance, London, this journal provides a wide range of knowledge and understanding of Islamic banking and insurance companies currently operating in about thirty countries. For subscription information, contact: *New Horizon*, 144–6 Kings Cross Road, London WC1X 9DH, UK.

Periodica Islamica (4 times a year; ISSN 0128-3715)
Published by Berita Publishing, this journal reproduces tables of contents from a wide variety of international serials, periodicals and other recurring publications. Also lists the titles of Islamic economics journals, with the contents of most recent issues. For subscription information, contact: Head, Research and Development Division, Berita Publishing, 22 Jalan Liku, 59100 Kuala Lumpur, Malaysia.

Review of Islamic Economics (1991–; twice a year; ISSN 0962-2055)
Published in English and Arabic by the International Association for Islamic Economics, this journal provides a forum to the specialist wishing to contribute to the development of Islamic economics. Major

areas of interest include: theoretical issues in economics from an Islamic perspective; empirical studies about the economics of modern countries; applied Islamic economics, e.g. Islamic banking; and survey articles in various fields of Islamic economics. Also contains book reviews. For subscription information, contact: Managing Editor, *Review of Islamic Economics*, Markfield Dawah Centre, Ratby Lane, Markfield, Leicester LE6 9RN, UK.

Thoughts on Economics (1980–; 4 times a year; ISSN 0256-8586)
Published by the Islamic Economics Research Bureau, this journal aims to undertake research on the economics of Islam with special reference to modern economic theory and practice. It publishes articles on Islamic economics, general economics and Bangladesh economics. Also contains book reviews, abstracts and short notes. For subscription information, contact: Executive Editor, *Thoughts on Economics*, Islamic Economics Research Bureau, PO Box 3966, Dhaka 1000, Bangladesh.

AUTHOR INDEX

SUBJECT INDEX